HOW TO BE THE GREATEST IMPROVISER ON EARTH

By Will Hines

ISBN 978-0-9826257-2-9 | © 2016 Pretty Great Publishing

CONTENTS

PREFACE

When I say "improv comedy," I mean: the art of making up comedy scenes as you go, on a stage. A group of people get on a stage, ask for a single suggestion, and then create one or more comedic scenes based on the suggestion. Generally, it looks like a comedic play.

The Compass Players pioneered this style of improv in Chicago during the 1950s, and it has flourished in the decades since through theaters like Second City, iO, and the Upright Citizens Brigade, among others.

You knew that, right? You better, or this book is just going to get more confusing from here.

INTRODUCTION

The problem with writing a book on doing improv comedy is that once you start thinking about it, all the advice starts to shrink.

It seems that improv advice really wants to be small. I try to write something grand and transformative, but once I get it down and revise it even a little bit, everything reduces to taut little mantras and tips. "Follow the fear." "Play to the top of your intelligence." "If this is true, then what else is true?"

There's something humble and pragmatic about small pieces of advice, which I like. They're little fistfuls of ideas you can carry with you on stage and shove up into your brain, without their taking up too much room. Isn't that all you need? After all, if you really want to get better as an improviser, you don't want a grand sermon so much as a few good tips—to get you over the hump of a bad scene until everything starts to click.

Improv is not that complicated, really. You just listen to each other and make up a funny scene. Here's every good improv scene:

1. Do something inspired by a suggestion.

2. Understand each other.

3. Move the scene forward.

4. Find/do something funny.

5. Do more of the funny thing.

Everything else that someone tells you must happen is either just semantics or taste.

Still, good improv scenes always feel so much grander than what a small piece of advice looks like.

I remember well the first truly good moment I had on stage. I'd been on one of the house teams at my theater for just over a year (yes, it took a year for me to feel I had a truly good moment). In the scene, Santa Claus had discovered his elves were actually robots, and they were mysteriously shutting down.

I was watching from the backline and felt a stirring that I should be an evil villain who had masterminded this scheme. Rather than thinking too much about it, or trying to figure out what my character's whole plan was, or even crafting an initial funny thing to say, I simply imagined myself into an evil being, stepped into the scene, and found myself saying: "Ha, ha, ha, Santa Claus!"

And the damnedest thing happened, which had never really happened to me before: the audience laughed. Hard.

What surprised me was that there didn't seem to be anything special about my move. There wasn't a joke, or impressive specificity, or anything particularly clever or surprising.

But there was something in that move: It was spontaneous, simple, committed, connected, and lively. It felt... real. Something stirred in my gut: *oh my God, I'm doing it. I'm doing improv, and I'm doing it right.*

With hindsight, I can see that the stirring in my gut was the sense of being truly present. I wasn't trying to solve the scene or force an ending. I was simply doing what the moment seemed to call for, based on the moments right before. It was good partly because it was so little. It was vulnerable and without an agenda.

You get into improv because you like comedy, but in moments like that you feel much more than simply funny. You feel connected to a flow. You're not thinking; you're just reacting and keeping an invisible ball in the air. When you hear a deep laugh from an audience like that, it doesn't just sound like they're saying, "That was funny." It sounds like they're saying, "We see you. You are true. You are real."

My first truly good moment was a small moment. But contained within it was a deeply rooted feeling of being what I'd always dreamed: a comedian.

It's powerful and addictive, that feeling. It's what we're all chasing when we do improv. Small, unplanned moments that feel connected to something grand.

SMALL BUT GRAND

The famous, bedrock improv mantra "Yes and" is a perfect example of a small statement with a larger truth. At first glance, it's just practical advice for how to improvise a scene without a script. You agree with the information and add to it.

But we improvisers know there is a far more ambitious mandate buried in that phrase. We hear that word "yes," and we know we're being asked to be brave and adventurous, not just in our scenes but in our whole lives. We hear the word "and," and we know we're being told to make a decision, to take a stand, not to be satisfied with simply watching things go by.

So many improv sayings sound like directives for your life:

- "Why is today important?"
- "Treat the audience like poets and geniuses."
- "Speak to the most important thing."
- "Don't be coy."
- "Find the love."

That's why people who love improv obsess as much about the teaching of it as the doing of it. You can use a mantra like "if this is true, then what else is true?" as a simple tool, or puzzle over its deeper meaning as if it were a Zen koan.

WHAT DOES IMPROV TEACH YOU?

In writing this book, I've thought back over my early years of improvising and tried to place myself back on the stage, to remember the way it felt. What were the big breakthrough moments, like the one where I became Santa Claus's villain, when I could really feel improv changing me and giving me new strengths and abilities?

Here is my list of lessons. If you practice improv, you will learn to:

- Be Present

- Be Changeable

- Fight Well

- Be Brave

- Play with Difficult People

- Be Authentic

- Be Funny

- Be Healthy

These are the principles that get at the heart of what makes improv special. These are skills that the real world burns out of you. You're socialized to think ahead, stay rigid, be careful, and often be false. Many are never taught to be funny or healthy.

This book includes exercises to help practice these skills. Some are classic, and others were developed by me or another teacher I know. Of course it's very easy to come up with similar exercises independently, so perhaps you have already run across similar ones.

There are many examples of real scenes throughout this book. I went to shows, recorded the scenes, and then transcribed them. I occasionally leave out a few lines, but generally I've tried to depict the scenes as they happened. This means the examples aren't perfect. They wander off topic, and players change their minds and adjust, or sometimes digress away from the main point of the scene. But these imperfections make the scenes feel immediate. They give the scenes a feeling of danger. I left them like this so you can get a feel for how scenes really play out.

Depending on where you are in your improv development, you'll probably find some of the lessons in this book helpful and others not so much. Then if you check back after a little while, you'll find different ones helpful than you did before. I ask that you try them on loosely. Sometimes you'll be looking for practical tips, and other times for a grand ambitious mantra. Almost everything in here can be either.

SOME
TERMS

This book is not going to teach you the basics of doing improv. It assumes you've studied the fundamentals, either through a theater or another book. But even the most basic terms can vary from theater to theater, so let's explicitly define a few phrases and make sure we're on the same page.

YES AND

This is the big one, the one that everyone knows. It's the mantra that explains how to do improv. On a practical level it means: when you are doing improv, you confirm the information that has already been said, then add more.

DENIAL

This refers to either an out-and-out rejection of something stated as fact (e.g., "Put down the phone? But I'm holding a sandwich!") or the rejection of the implied, unstated context of something ("You want me to dance? But this is a restaurant!"). Denial is a cardinal sin, despite the unfortunate truth that it can be extremely funny, which is why very veteran teams indulge in selectively denying their scene partners.

TOP OF YOUR INTELLIGENCE

This means, "Don't make your character dumber than he should be." All things being equal, you play your characters as smart people who know as much as you would know in that situation. Lots of people, when they feel the pressure to be funny, make their character arbitrarily stupid. Now, there's plenty of time for selective stupidity—where there's a method to the madness—but don't be broadly dumb just to get things going.

THE UNUSUAL THING / GAME OF THE SCENE

"Game of the scene" is a term coined by the Upright Citizens Brigade, and it means (very roughly) "the funny part." The funny part starts when we find something that's different from what we expect: "the unusual thing."

There's the real world and how things normally go—that's the scene. And then there's a weird part that is unusual—that's the game.

If you improvise a boxing manager who tells fighters to never throw punches, then the boxing match is the scene, and the manager's insane advice is the game. The two fighters shake hands, someone rings a bell, the fighters dance to the center—that's the scene. And then one drops his arms to his sides and lets himself get hit in the face, because that's what his manager told him to do—that's the game.

There are many semantic arguments about the "game of the scene." That's because the game addresses the comedy of the scene, and analyzing comedy with terms and categories is a dicey, imperfect business. The most common argument is over the difference between "an unusual thing" and a "full game," which is an unusual thing heightened and explored.

For the purposes of this book, a game is the unusual thing. What you do with it, how long you play with it, and how far you take it are all matters of taste.

When we use the term "game of the scene" and emphasize its importance in this book, it is because we are presupposing that we want our improv scenes to have a funny part and not just be dramatic scenes. Was it funny? Then it had a game.

Funny improvisers can be said to "get game."

JUSTIFYING / SAYING WHY

Improv scenes often involve someone doing or saying unusual things. Very often the character with the unusual behavior will be challenged to answer, "Why are you doing this?" We call explaining your weird behavior "justifying." It's usually not a sensible explanation, and it may be something that makes sense only to someone looking at the situation from an odd perspective. See this scene between James Mannion and Cory Jacob.

> **James:** Roger, why did you write your reports in blood?

> **Cory:** I wanted you to know I care about this company.

IF THIS IS TRUE, THEN WHAT ELSE IS TRUE?

Once you have something funny, you ask, "If this is true, then what else is true?" If a priest decides that he is an atheist, maybe we see a scene where his choir has been instructed to sing the R.E.M. song "Losing My Religion." What else might he do? Perhaps he's replaced the crucifixes with statues of Albert Einstein.

Answering this line of questioning in your scenes is also called "playing the game."

SUGGESTION / INITIATION / WALK-ONS / TAGS / EDITS

Suggestion: Most long-form improv sets begin with a word or a phrase from a member of the audience. This serves as the jumping-off point for the start of the set, not necessarily as a major topic to be explored.

Initiation: The first line of a scene.

Walk-On: An entrance into a scene already in motion, i.e., by someone other than the people who started the scene.

Tag: An improv convention in which an actor who has not been in a scene walks up to and taps a character on the shoulder. The person who is tapped leaves, and is replaced by the new person. Whoever else was not tapped remains. It's implied that, once the new person enters, the scene changes to a new location (related in some way to the original scene).

For example, let's say we have a job interviewer who is yelling at an applicant. An improviser who has not been in the scene walks up and tags the applicant. The applicant leaves. The new improviser takes his place and addresses the interviewer, "I understand you've been yelling at our applicants." It's implied that we have moved into the future, and now the interviewer is getting scolded by his manager.

Edits: An agreed-upon convention for players to signal to each other that a scene is finished. The most typical edit is the "sweep," where one player runs across the front of the stage, as if a curtain is being closed.

GIFTS / ENDOWMENTS / PIMPS

Gift / Endowment: When someone declares something new about another actor's character, it's a gift. "You look happy." When you essentially assign someone a role, it's an endowment. "You must be my father." Gifts and endowments are good, and those terms are often used interchangeably.

Pimp: A pimp is when you go too far and you make it so your scene partner has to perform a stunt. "Weren't you going to read a poem? In Spanish?"

DEL CLOSE / OPENINGS / SECOND BEATS / HAROLDS / CONNECTIONS

Del Close: An improv director in Chicago during the 1960s–1990s, who championed long-form improv as a performance art and not just a tool in rehearsals.

An Opening: A ritual where you take a suggestion and expand it into ideas. It should feel like an overture before a musical, in that you hear snippets of ideas to be expanded upon later. They are artsy, abstract, and hard, and there are many different kinds.

Second Beat: During a set of multiple scenes, a second beat occurs when your scene revisits characters or a situation from an earlier scene in the show. Usually you try to revisit whatever made the original scene unique, rather than just continue the story. If you are revisiting a scene for a second time that's called a "third beat."

The Harold: An improv structure developed by Del Close when he worked with Charna Halpern at the iO Theatre in Chicago. Played strictly, it goes like this: suggestion, opening, three scenes, group scene, three second beats, group scene, three third beats.

Connections: When characters or ideas from one scene show up in a later scene that had been otherwise unrelated. When the various stories of a sitcom overlap at the end of an episode, they are "connecting."

Now that we have our terms, let's get into the skills you need to take your improv to a higher level.

BE PRESENT

If you were to take the fear that a new improviser feels, tear it from her soul, and condense it into a sentence, it would be this: "What do I say next?"

Next. Later. The ending. New improvisers are constantly looking ahead, trying to see a clear path to a nice, satisfying ending.

You're going to have to forget that.

An important step of becoming a great improviser is letting go of the future and choosing to BE PRESENT.

And all you need to do in order to be present is to ignore one of the most basic human instincts you have: you need to stop thinking ahead.

If you are a human being who has survived past the age of zero, you are not great at being present. You wake up, and you're already worried about when you're going to get to the post office to pick up that package, or what you're going to get for your friend's birthday on Thursday, or if you'll have something cool to say at your 50th high school reunion in 20 years.

Someone walks up to you at work and says hello, and you immediately start scrutinizing her face to guess what's coming next: "What the heck does this person want with me? Is she gonna try to get me to sign a birthday card? Is it too late for me to pretend to not see her? Also, what am I gonna say at my 50th high school reunion in 20 years?"

As soon as you start watching a movie, you're trying to guess the ending. When the TV goes out for one second, you're picking which relative you're going to rescue if it turns out that a zombie uprising has started.

As soon as you've decided that you are going to ask someone out, you start wondering what kind of couple you'd be, how long you might last, how many children you'd have.

You won't be fooled, your instincts assure you. You will be ahead of it, way ahead.

But the present moment is huge in improv because improv happens on a **stage**. The audience are people who are in the same room as you. They can hear your breathing. They can see every little change on your face. They can pick up on every little piece of nonverbal information you're putting out there. If you hear your ex-girlfriend in the audience sigh, your eyebrows will perk just slightly higher, and the whole audience will know that something is up.

There is always a lot going on in the current moment if you're practiced at paying attention to it, but new improv students are always worried about the future. A new improv student looks at their scene partner and thinks: *Maybe my character is going to fall in love with this other character.* They make that choice. *I'll start planting seeds now that we will someday be in love.* And they say out loud, warmly, "Nice day, isn't it?"

Meaning: nothing is happening now, and the scene is dying. The student is setting up a moment that isn't here yet. In fact, it won't ever get here.

Instead, you must see what is already happening and report it. Like this:

- You're sitting down at a table, so you decide you must be at a restaurant, and begin miming that you're eating. That's happening now.

- Roughly at the same time, you see your partner is smiling at you, so you feel that you must be on a date and you smile back. *Ooh, something is afoot.*

- You notice that in doing this you feel kindly to the other character, so you think, *maybe I'm in love with this person.* And out loud you say "I love you," to let your scene partner know what you're thinking. You just get right to it, so that it's happening in front of the audience's eyes.

- And because your scene partner was watching your eyes, he/she knows how your character feels, looks down and takes the moment in, and then looks up and says, "I wish I felt the same way."

When you are present, you report what is happening. You are always in the middle of the moment. You feel it and make an assumption about what must already be happening, which also means, by the way, that you always assume something is happening. When someone says "hi," it's never just "hi."

You shrink your scope down. Instead of thinking ahead 22 minutes, or even two minutes, you look around you at the current moment.

"Now" gets bigger and slower and richer and more evident.

You turn into a Sherlock Holmes of observing the present instant. From a snapshot of a moment, you can make decisions about what you feel, what the other person must be feeling, and what must have happened to get us here.

It's not where you're driving, but what the car ride feels like now, what you feel about the passenger, the song on the radio, and the landscape you can see right at that moment.

You're constantly waking up into worlds that already exist and trying to fake it. There's no point in planning ahead, because everything is constantly changing.

You observe and react—honestly and directly—and wait for your partner to do the same, and then you'll have something else to observe and react to.

The future vanishes! It's weird and cool and oddly soothing.

BECOME THE MOST RIVETING PERSON ON THE STAGE

You will know that you are truly being present when this happens: you become the most riveting person on stage.

They say you can't teach charisma. But you can, and I just taught it to you.

Be fully present, and the audience will watch you like a hawk.

It doesn't matter how good an actor you are. Or how "naturally charismatic" you are. If you are honestly communicating how the current moment feels, in an authentic way—no matter how clumsily or awkwardly—the audience will pay attention to you. People will magically give you space. Yes. It happens.

I saw a show a million years ago with a nervous, bulldogging man and a quiet, confident woman. He started the scene as a husband on a fishing trip with his wife. He was complaining about the weather and demanding a beer and asking her why she picked this day to go fishing, all the while not giving her time to answer. She had time only to peep things like no and yes and "Boy, it sure is rainy!"

In his defense, the guy was more nervous than actually bullying, but the effect was that his scene partner couldn't get a word out.

But she was so much more confident as an actor! She did everything physically. Her eyebrows popped up when he revealed that the weather was bad. She looked a bit sad when he said the fish weren't gonna bite. When he asked for a beer, she leaned over into a cooler and plucked a beer up in sharp, funny movements. I remember she clutched the can just at the top with her fingertips, letting the imaginary can dangle as if it were a gross thing she didn't want to touch. And when she handed it over to him, and he absent-mindedly took it as he rambled, she gave a quick nod of satisfaction to herself, and at that the audience laughed.

She was in the scene. She was a specific character. She was cool and calm and confident and specific. She was having fun. She was funnier.

And all the while he was talking, we were just watching her.

That woman? MERYL STREEP. No, I'm kidding. I don't know who she was. But I remember thinking that's the way to play with a stage hog: you ride the wave in front of you, instead of looking ahead for a different one.

SEE IT LAND, LET IT LAND

A good note for being present is *see it land, let it land.*

You make a move—verbal or non-verbal—and wait to see it land in your partner's face before you keep going. That's "see it land."

And when your partner makes a move, you feel it and show your feelings. Just a bit. A little smile, a little nod. That's "let it land."

Improv often feels like a series of couplets. You move, they move back. They move, you react. You both provoke reactions in each other, like two poles of a battery.

BE COMFORTABLE WITH SILENCE

Another obstacle to being present: people talk too much. New improvisers routinely talk until they are interrupted. They think talking equals confidence.

Stop talking. Let there be silence after you speak. That's when your words are absorbed.

Stop talking, maintain eye contact, and let stuff sink in.

REPS

Students in my classes will often ask for "hard notes." They want the hard truth on what they need to do to get better. I generally do not oblige.

The hard truth is often simply: learn to act like a normal person.

Ever see what happens to a person when you point a camera at them? Their face goes into a fake frozen smile. Their spine stiffens. I've seen people unconsciously bend their arms so they look like robots, and also inexplicably tilt their heads far to the side. And these are the changes that happen just for a still photograph, something we all actually have a decent amount of practice doing.

In improv we're asking you to move around, talk, and make things up, all while being watched. This is all before we even worry about being interesting, surprising, or funny. Just the basics of existing like a natural human being are incredibly difficult at first.

But these basics are essential if you want to be funny on stage. You have to look comfortable and natural in the unnatural world of an improvised scene.

Another challenge: people, in general, are bad at words. You have a feeling, and then your brain has to do some amount of work to miraculously translate that feeling into words. And then the recipient has to take those words and complete the even harder task of translating them back into feelings.

Recently in class I saw someone forget his own name. Remembering other people's names is very hard, I know, but I had assumed retrieving your own name from your brain would be simple. Still, during a names warm-up, one student, when he was supposed to say his own name, went, "Dave. Wait! No, I mean Sean."

He was flustered. It's the start of class, and he feels the weight of everyone watching him. Everyone is like that when they're learning. Even veterans are like that on certain days. Words are hard.

Another time I saw a scene that went like this:

Player 1: Could you keep it down? Your drums are really loud.

Player 2: I'm sorry. I just… it's that I have a gig tomorrow.

Player 1: You're keeping up my wife and infant son. What's your problem?

Player 2: Nothing! I mean, I love infants.

No one says, "I love infants." Maybe you say, "I love babies!" or "Babies are so cute." But no one in the course of a normal conversation says, "I love infants." For that matter, no one says, "You're keeping up my wife *and infant son.*"

Now, on one hand, that kind of awkward phrasing is part of the fun of improv. You word things slightly "wrong," and it's a gift you use to have fun on stage. But when you're starting out, almost every single thing you say is peppered with awkwardness. The unintentional game of every scene, when you are learning, is "these people sound insane."

It's normal. Your chords aren't wrong, you're just looking at the frets and taking a long time to get your fingers into place. You're heading down the court in the right direction, but you're looking at the ball while you dribble. The music starts, but you don't start dancing for several measures, and when you do you're behind the beat.

That's okay! You're learning.

But there's no hard note that gives you comfort on stage. No teacher, exercise, or book. It's just reps. Repeat, repeat, repeat. It is the most reliable method for getting better. More and more of your real self will become available to you as you keep at it.

BE PRESENT EXERCISES

60 SECONDS OF SILENCE

Think of your brain as an excited puppy, trying to race ahead to the future. Here's an exercise to get it back to the present.

Two people up. They get a suggestion and then assume a starting position. Something not too big is best—a hip cocked to one side is better than a big crouch while screaming. The people should be able to see each other. No stepping downstage and gazing out over the audience.

Then they wait 60 seconds. No object work. The scene isn't starting. They just wait 60 seconds and regard each other. After 60 seconds, the teacher says "start," and they do.

60 seconds on stage is a hugely long time. At first your brain is racing: you're thinking of ideas of how you might start the scene. You pick one. Then you don't like that idea and you change it. Then you're trying to guess what the other person is thinking, and you change your mind again. You become self-conscious about your posture and adjust it.

Then you start to settle. You're still thinking things, but it's less frantic. You start to settle on a vague, not-quite-locked-down notion of who you are and how you are feeling as a character. The self-consciousness and panic boils away. You relax.

Then, you're calm. You have a general sense of the dynamic—*I'm nervous; she's stern* or *I'm excited; he's also excited.* Ideas float into your brain, but now they're like pieces of paper gently floating on a breeze, not gunshots at your feet commanding you to dance.

And then the scene starts. You will be listening well for the first time.

Don't worry if the scenes begin a bit slowly. They will quickly become very compelling and good.

ONLY NUMBERS

Two people up. No suggestion. They do a scene where they only say numbers, in order, to each other.

So the first person says, "One."

And the other person responds, "Two, three, four?"

And the first person says, "Five! Six! Seven."

No repeating numbers. If someone goes "Eight?" you don't respond with "Eight." You respond with "Nine."

At first people will try to communicate very specific, very literal things. Someone will be trying to say, "I'm mad at my husband. He was supposed to meet me here!" but they can only say, "One! Two, three, four! Five!" They are gesticulating a ton and trying to make "two" equal "husband."

But that doesn't work. You can't re-use numbers, so there's no way to make any number mean anything. And we can't see your "husband," so there's no way to know that you're talking about him.

The other person can only tell that you're upset, so they adopt a soothing tone. "Six. Seven." They are trying to calm you down.

Then, you stop trying to make specific points. You just start responding to each other's tone. If "six" and "seven" are said in a soothing way, then you calm down and say, "Eight, nine, ten," in a sort of "you're right, you're right" tone.

Dialogue has a music to it, and that music communicates a lot. Being present means being in touch with that music.

Variation: Each person can only say one number. This forces you to use silence and tone to get feeling out of just one word.

DOING "ZIP ZAP ZOP" CORRECTLY

If ever there were an improv exercise that seems as if it doesn't need explaining, it's the classic Zip Zap Zop. It's the simplest of all improv warm-ups. Class stands in a circle. One person claps in the direction of someone else and says "zip." The person clapped at claps simultaneously with the clapper, then passes the motion on by clapping at someone else and saying "zap." And then that third person claps at someone else while saying "zop," and then that person claps at yet another someone and starts over with "zip."

The next time you do Zip Zap Zop, notice how often you are startled when you are clapped at.

Someone claps at you and says "zip," and you give a very small start. "Whoa," you quietly say before continuing the exercise by clapping and saying "zap." You had sunk into yourself and detached from the moment.

All that happens in this exercise is people saying "zip," "zap," and "zop," yet those actions continually surprise the people doing it.

This is what we're up against when we are trying to be present. Your mind is constantly trying to pull back from the current moment, sneak to somewhere deep inside yourself, and just watch.

But you need to be present, ready to respond. Bend your knees ever so slightly, lean forward, and be in it.

WARM-UP SCENES

This isn't even an exercise, but if you want to get better at being present, leave time at the start of every practice for a simple batch of warm-up scenes.

Everyone up. Two at a time, you do scenes. A new suggestion for each one. The coach calls "edit" after about a minute. No walk-ons, no tag-outs, no support—just a series of short, two-person scenes. No notes either. Just do a batch of scenes. You go until everyone has done two.

Allow yourself this time to warm up and get comfortable. I've never seen a class that didn't get better with 20 minutes of mostly uninterrupted scenes near the top of a practice.

WORD ASSOCIATION / FOLLOW THE FOLLOWER

Here's another simple exercise that will anchor you to the present moment. It's good for a warm-up at the top of a practice, before you start doing scenes.

Everyone gets up and forms a circle. Then there are two parts.

First part is "word association." The teacher picks someone to start. That person points at someone else in the circle and says any word or phrase ("traffic light," "stone," "acceptance"). That person then points at someone else and says whatever that term makes them think of.

Specific ("suitable match," "ferocious appearance," "south of France") is better than general, but it's more important to just keep it moving.

Second part is "follow the follower." After about 20 seconds of word association, someone in the group makes a big physical move—preferably in reaction to whatever was just said at that moment, though it's more important to just do it when it needs to be done. If someone has just said "carpentry," then someone else might make a hammering gesture and make the sound "clang."

Once the person has made a physical move, everyone switches into a non-verbal "follow the follower." That means everyone just physically copies each other so that the whole group is repeating a physical action. The group continues to copy each other, letting the group's action morph quickly and easily. (I describe "follow the follower" in more detail in the "Be Brave" chapter).

Then, after about 20 seconds of physical movement, someone stands up straight and points and says a word or phrase. The whole group snaps back into a circle and does word association again. After 20 more seconds, some one makes a big physical move: back to follow the follower.

Alternate "words" mode with "physical" mode for roughly four minutes.

By alternating between verbal/analytical skills and non-verbal/physical/ animal skills. this exercise helps you integrate the responses of your logical left brain and your more intuitive right brain. The two sides inform each other. When the group finishes their first physical round and returns to words, they will be energized and the choices will come more easily. Once they come back to the physical, after words, they will be more specific and fluid with their physical choices.

You'll be focused on the present, no longer thinking ahead.

BE
CHANGEABLE

I have a completely unfair test that I try on people to see if they would be good improvisers.

I offer the person a mundane thing, like a piece of gum or a glass of water, or even a pen. "Hey, want a glass of water?" or "I'm going to go get a sandwich—you want anything?" (If the person says yes, then I can't do the test, and I just give them the gum or whatever.)

But if the person says no, I immediately ask, "Why, are you scared?"

This test is funny because most people will instinctively say, "What? No, I'm not scared." They say this even though the question does not make any sense. Of course they are not scared of gum. Really what they are saying is: "I don't quite know what you mean by that question, and in fact I don't really know what's going on, but I will tell you this much: I am not scared."

People who are naturally good at improv will instinctively adjust themselves to the absurdity of the question. They say, "Yes, I am scared." Or maybe they'll say, "Yes, very scared, in fact." Really good ones will change their face to actually look a little scared.

They just adapt themselves for the fun of it.

If someone does that, and they've never studied improv, I will tell them, "You should take an improv class. You'd be great at it." And they're like, "Were we talking about improv?" And I say, "No, and also I don't have any gum."

This section is about being changeable. It is a skill uniquely important to being an improviser. All actors learn to be present, but the improviser also becomes equally adept at being changeable.

WHAT MUST HAVE ALREADY HAPPENED?

One of the keys to being changeable is making this switch: every time you worry, "What is going to happen next?" replace it with, "What must have already happened?"

Stop looking forward and start thinking about the moment before.

Here's a scene between actors Dennis Curlett and Danny Cymbal. They start as co-workers talking in a break room, and work backwards from the way they are talking to each other to create the scene.

> **Dennis:** Hey, buddy, what's going on with you?

> **Danny:** Oh, Phil, hi! I'm just taking a quick break before I gotta get back and type all the reports up. How's Mary?

> **Dennis:** She's great! She made a lasagna.

> **Danny:** Oh yeah?

> **Dennis:** Yeah! Like a meatball lasagna.

> **Danny:** And um, don't tell me. Tim. Little Tim, how is he?

Dennis decides here that the reason Danny's character is naming everyone in Dennis's character's life is to passive-aggressively make the point that he, Dennis, does not know *Danny's* name. Once Dennis declares this, Danny agrees to it.

Dennis: Okay, I know what you're doing. Yeah, I don't remember your name.

Danny: Yeah.

Dennis: Okay, I'm sorry. I apologize.

Danny: It hurts. Okay?

Dennis: It's kinda freaky to me how much information you retain about MY life.

Danny: I do it on purpose!

Dennis: What?

Danny: Because you never remember, man!

Dennis: It's not a personal thing, man!

Danny: It's not a personal thing? We've hung out!

Dennis: Okay, it's just one thing doesn't stick in my head.

Danny: My name? What is it?

Dennis hesitates. Danny starts to say his character's own name, to give Dennis a hint.

Danny: Daaa—

Dennis: Dave!

Danny: You didn't remember.

Dennis: No, I didn't! I didn't! I'm sorry, I'm just a guy who's bad with names. Look, you're obviously important to me because I still hang out with you! I started this conversation with YOU. I'm just bad with names!

Danny: Whatever. Cool. We're fine. It's fine.

Dennis: No, no, okay, look. How about for the next six months you can call me anything you want.

Danny: How does that make it better?

Dennis: I don't know! I just feel bad! I want you to know it's not a personal thing. It's a problem I have, and for the next six months you can call me anything you want and I will answer to it.

Danny: That's fine, we're fine, that's good. Don't worry.

Dennis: All right. I'm sorry.

Danny: *(leading him)* Sorry...?

Dennis: Sorry....

Danny: It was literally three seconds ago I told you my name.

Dennis: You really think I don't remember your name right now?

Danny: Yes, I really think you don't remember my name right now.

Dennis: Well, you are 100% correct. I don't know!

Keith Johnstone said, "Improvisation is like steering a car by looking through the rear view mirror."

The future is not worth worrying about in improv, especially when you're at the start of a scene. You only need to worry about adjusting and confirming—letting the other people in the scene know that you know what's going on.

Another example. Let's say you're playing a girlfriend on a date in a park. After a few lines, your boyfriend drops to his knees and says, "Will you marry me?"

You might be tempted to play it that your character is completely surprised by this. After all, you, the actor, are completely surprised, and it would be reasonable for the character to be surprised.

But a more sophisticated move would be, the moment you see him proposing, you adjust your thinking to: this relationship is not new, it has been going on for a long time, and now he's proposing. You might not have known it was coming now, but you probably knew it was coming at some point. You're probably at a stage where every time you go on a trip with your significant other, you are wondering if this is when he's going to propose.

The funniest and most apt response when the boyfriend drops to his knees and proposes is not "I can't believe it!" but "Finally!"

BE COMMITTED, NOT ATTACHED

One of the main tenets of good acting and good improvising is to commit. Be invested in your character. Really believe in the things your character believes.

But the trick is that you also must be ready, always, to shift and adjust.

I read an interview with baseball player Alex Rodriguez, in which he said that right before he swings his bat, he's holding it very lightly. He said that if someone were to grab the bat one second before the pitch, they'd be able to easily snatch it out of his grasp. It isn't until just before he's about to swing that he tightens his grip—yet it looks from the outside as if he's holding the bat firmly the entire time.

That's how your choices should be: confident and convincing to the observer, but ready for rapid adjustment at any moment.

I once saw this scene between improvisers Jesse Falcon and Jason Mantzoukas. Jesse bursts through a door, and Jason is sitting at a desk. Jesse says, "Come quick! There's a monster in the swamp!" And Jason very quickly shoots back with, "I. Don't. Care!" He says it firmly, confidently. It is very funny for him to blow off Jesse like that, and the audience laughs.

It's also an overtly bad improv move. He's ignoring the initiation, which is basically a denial. And he really laid that denial out there and got a laugh off of it. This could break the scene, by creating a precedent that nothing said is really happening.

But Jason adjusts. He realizes he's threatened the scene, sighs, and says, "But... I am the sheriff. Let's go check it out." He mimes reaching into a desk and pulling out a badge.

Problem fixed! No harm done. If he had stuck rigidly to "I don't care!" as hard as he first made that choice, that scene would have died. He adjusted.

Make big choices and commit, but be ready to change.

KEEP THE MUSIC, CHANGE THE LYRICS

What if you have to change in a way that contradicts something you've already done? Isn't that going to break the scene?

Not really. A common strategy is to keep the tone you have, and just change the things you talk about. Keep the music, change the lyrics.

Here's what I mean:

Let's say you mime heaving open double saloon doors and walking with heavy boots, implying that you are a cowboy entering a saloon. Then someone greets you, "Hello, Principal. Your 10 a.m. appointment is waiting."

They don't do it as a joke; they just missed what you did. You have two options:

1. If you haven't yet spoken, you could just drop your physicality totally and switch into the body language of a principal. The audience might giggle, or they might not even notice. If your scene partner didn't see it, maybe it wasn't as big a deal as you thought. Getting on the same page is more important.

2. If you have already spoken, you can keep the tone of your voice and the physicality, but agree with the new choice.

So, if you mime heaving open double doors and say, "Charlie, get me a whiskey" in a gruff voice—and then someone says, "Principal Davis, your 10 a.m. is waiting for you"—you just nod and keep walking the way you're walking and say, "Great. Thanks, Morris. Bring me the attendance reports, and dammit, Charlie, get me that whiskey!"

You keep the music, and just change the lyrics. You can easily fold changes into your scene that way.

EVERY LINE IS AN OFFER

One of my teachers, Michael Delaney, has a good piece of advice: "Good improvisers habitually agree with offers made to them."

"Agree with offers" means that you choose to view things that happen in the scene as offers, and that you generally want to accept them.

It's like "yes and" but a bit more pointed.

If someone says to your character, "Hey, you look angry," a good improviser tends to want to make that true. Notice the "tend"—you don't have to go with it. If it directly contradicts something that is a big part of your character, you can sidestep it, but your general default instinct should be to go with it.

If someone says, "Man, what a view," you see that as an offer to talk about the view.

Accepting offers is really important at the top of the scene. It counteracts our instincts to add in too much that belongs only to us. Slow down, absorb everything, adjust your thinking, and say yes.

It's not as important once the scene gets rolling and we all have points of view and things to unpack. At that time, too much accepting offers can stall the scene.

A side note that we'll talk more about later, in the section on fighting well in scenes: telling someone not to do something is an offer to do it more. If someone says, "Would you stop being so rude to my father?" they want you to be rude to their father. The most helpful thing for you to do in that example is to turn to the father immediately and say, "You look like a troll."

HALF-OFFERS

Lots of times in scenes, someone will say, "Is this about...?" It's what I call a half-offer. You should consider it, but you don't have to accept it. See this scene between improvisers Lisa Timmons and Gwen Mesco.

Lisa: I cut my own hair this morning. And I don't know what to do, should I... how does it look?

Gwen: I feel like, when I've had bad haircuts, I don't want people to lie to me when it happens, and it's not good.

Lisa: Okay, I accept the fact that it doesn't look great.

Gwen: It does *not* look great. But you're still very pretty. You have really good bone structure. I just moved to this neighborhood that has a lot of Orthodox Jews, and they have a lot of wig stores.

Lisa: Let's get a wig then!

Gwen: Yeah, let's get a wig.

Lisa: Do you have any? Do you just… happen to have some?

Gwen: Is this about Joe?

In that last sentence Gwen is making a half-offer to Lisa.

Some teachers suggest that you always take these, unless they directly contradict something we already know. But sometimes people will offer an "is this about…?" that is so far afield of what's happening it would derail the scene, such as:

- "Is this about how you really want to have sex?"
- "Is this about how you resent me?"
- "Is this about you hating your kids?"

If the half-offer is nowhere close to what you are thinking and feeling, it's okay to reject it, though it's good form to yes-and some part of it, if you can:

- "In the past, this has been about sex. But right now that's not at all what I'm thinking about."
- "I do sometimes resent you, but not right now."
- "My kids drive me nuts, but I don't hate them."

Think of these half-offers as similar to when someone offers you food at a party. Accepting it is gracious, and dismissing it without even thinking about it is rude. But if you're allergic to this particular food or really full—it's okay to politely decline.

In the scene between Lisa and Gwen, Lisa accepted the half-offer that her hair crisis was really about a breakup.

> **Lisa:** So you saw that Instagram. She has short hair!

> **Gwen:** I know! So what? We all know you can do better than him!

EMPATHY

Underlying the skill of being changeable is empathy. It's the ability to see where someone else is coming from. To be fluid. To adopt points of view you not only weren't expecting, but that you don't agree with and barely understand. To change your own character's history instantly, in order to make the current moment make sense.

Empathy in an improv scene is not easy. People struggle to accept gifts if it means having opinions they wouldn't naturally have.

But if you're being changeable, you need to do it.

Someone endows you as Adolf Hitler? You have to embody the mindset of Hitler, from his point of view, as best you can assume. He didn't see himself as a crazy person. He probably saw himself as a capable guy who wasn't afraid to call out the truth, or to make grand plans and really "go for it." He was probably proud of generally winning at everything he did, as that is kind of what happened right up until the end.

Of course I am not saying Hitler was good. Let me go on record here: I am opposed to Adolf Hitler. But if I get endowed as him in a scene, then I'm going to play even him with a degree of empathy.

Empathy gets ignored when people wax nostalgic about the powers of improv. Everyone focuses instead on the lesson of "saying yes." Even accomplished comedians look back at their time in improv and speak about the revolutionary concept of being cooperative, and how their lives were so beautifully improved when they started learning how to "say yes" to things.

But it's the ability to change your viewpoint to something you did not expect, with truthfulness and ease, that is the game-changing skill you develop as an improviser. You can make any position truthful.

Here are a few feats of empathy that improv will require you to perform on stage, from easiest to hardest.

1. *Being an intelligent version of a character who believes something you do not.* If you're a passionate liberal, can you play a right-wing politician with strident religious beliefs and not sound like a jerk? Can you set aside your distaste for that person and indeed advocate for them?

2. *Yes-anding a character that your character disagrees with, without changing your character's mind.* If you're a right-wing religious zealot, and the other character is someone trying to legalize heroin, can you say something like, "I remember how you took that economics class, and it convinced you legalizing drugs was a smart idea—but it's not worth it. It's morally wrong"? In other words, can you hold onto one viewpoint while furthering a different one?

3. *Yes-anding an accusation lobbed at your character that genuinely surprises you, the actor.* If you're a right-wing religious zealot, and someone says to you, "That never stopped you from shoplifting from my store," can you accept that and justify it with ease, even if seems at first to be contradictory to your character? "I steal to protect the free market, which is a way of honoring God." A non-empathetic move would be to fight back and counter-accuse the other character as a way of trying to "win" the scene. "I only stole because you had slept with my wife!"

4. *Yes-anding the other character while justifying an accusation that surprised you.* Let's say you respond to "That never stopped you from shoplifting from my store" with "You're good at noticing people's hypocrisy. I admire that in you." I bet it would get a laugh, just for being a surprisingly generous response.

Other handy tricks that empathy lets you do:

- Being able to respond to what someone meant to say, rather than quibble over the wording of what they actually said.

- Speaking to the suggestion in a way the audience intended you to. If someone suggests "snowstorm" during a week of an actual snowstorm, they are thinking of different aspects of a snowstorm than someone who gives that suggestion in July.

- Giving endowments to other actors that they are happy to receive. Giving gifts people want.

And for what it's worth, the ability to see things from someone else's point of view comes in handy in real life far more often than a willingness to "say yes" to situations you'd normally avoid.

BEING CHANGEABLE EXERCISES

CHARACTER MATCHING

Everyone in a circle. The teacher picks someone to start. That person walks across the circle and speaks as a character for a line or two.

Perhaps they adopt the tone of an elderly, crotchety man, and say, "Well, look who's playing in my yard! The Spencer boy!"

Whoever is being spoken to responds as the same kind of character. Same voice, same philosophy. Even in this case, when it has been established that the person being spoken to is a little boy, the little boy responds in the same voice and philosophy.

"That's me! What a troublemaker I am! And I'm gonna mess up your lawn good!"

The initiator responds, making this a three-line scene: "You better not!"

Then the person who crossed the circle takes the responder's spot, and the responder walks across the circle and speaks as a brand-new character to someone else.

This exercise lets you quickly adopt a variety of energies, and lets you practice changing yourself based on someone else's decisions.

This is an exercise from teacher Corey Brown to practice giving and receiving offers.

Two people up. Give one a playing card (or a business card or even a scrap of paper). Then give them a suggestion. Either person can start regardless of who has the card.

Continue the scene until the person with the card makes any kind of an offer.

"Man, I'm beat," or
"You look happy," or
"Nice weather outside."

Or a more indirect one, like, "John, get in my office," which implies they're at work and that the other person works for him, probably.

At that point—when the person with the card adds something—he passes the card to the other person. The card represents his offer. When the person takes the card, he must explicitly accept the offer.

"You look tired all right," or
"I AM feeling pretty good!" or
"Yeah, look at that blue sky," or
(as John) "Sure, Bill, here I'll close the door."

Simple is better. The response should just confirm the information.

Then you keep going until the person who now has the card makes another offer. Then she passes the card back, and the person taking it explicitly confirms that offer.

It's not essential that the person who takes the card agrees with an opinion. If the person says "This job sucks," and passes a card, you could take the card and say, "I know—you really hate it here."

Let the card go back and forth five or six times.

After you do this exercise, you will notice scenes where someone is constantly repeating the same information again and again, as if they are trying to pass a card to their scene partner. If they're repeating themselves, it's time for the other person to accept the offer, or else the person just needs to adjust and drop it to talk about something else.

LA RONDE

This is a common form or exercise, but here we're going to do it with a focus on being changeable.

Basic structure

The basic structure is inspired by an old play called, yes, *La Ronde*, where every scene has two characters, one of whom was in the previous scene. The actual play is about sexual politics in 1890s Vienna, with scene titles like "The Whore and The Soldier" followed by "The Soldier and the Parlor Maid."

The improv version just borrows the structure and not the focus on sexual politics. If you have five people, it goes like this:

First scene has Person A and Person B

Next scene has Person B and Person C.

Next scene has Person C and Person D.

Next scene has Person D and Person E.

Final scene has Person E and Person A.

It creates a sort of circle.

You don't pick ahead of time who does which scene, and you don't pick which character. You get a suggestion, and then two people just step out and do a scene. After a few minutes, someone tags out one of the two. Whoever is tagged out becomes Person A and stays on the back line until the last scene.

1. Everyone should try to be a simple character with a simple "thing," meaning one of the following:

   a. you're a very familiar **archetype** (e.g., "schoolteacher" or "drill sergeant");

   b. you have a clear **point of view** ("perky idealist" or "grouch who hates young people"); or

   c. you have a clear **emotional temperament** ("cheery" or "sad").

2. Then, whenever someone tags in, your goal is to put the character from the previous scene into a place that we would never expect to see them. If the first scene is a drill sergeant yelling at a soldier, someone could tag in as a yoga teacher—and thus we see the angry drill sergeant in a yoga class, i.e., a situation we would not expect for that character.

Everyone ends up doing two scenes. You stay the same character in each of your scenes. It's implied that everyone lives in the same universe, though that may not matter.

Focus on being changeable

The trick here is that when the character gets put in the new situation, they must like it. They still behave the same way they did in the previous scene, and the actor comes up with a reason why they like this situation.

If you're the drill sergeant who was yelling and screaming at the soldier, and then you're in a yoga class, you do the poses with the same angry grunting and yelling that you did in the previous scene. You have some reason why you like yoga. You're not surprised to be there, and you don't say you're being forced to do it.

Meanwhile the yoga teacher is being very typical for a yoga teacher, talking in a soothing voice, moving in a slow, fluid way. Then the drill sergeant gets tagged out, and we see the yoga teacher at a heavy metal concert with a heavy metal fan. The yoga teacher loves it and waves his body around and cheers happily in a very soothing way for the heavy metal band.

If this seems hard, it's not. In real life, we often focus on the parts of an experience which we relate to, and ignore the rest. Maybe the drill sergeant is really into the discipline of yoga, and just doesn't pay attention to the peaceful aspect of it. Maybe the yoga teacher likes the "inner truth" of heavy metal and doesn't pay attention to all the violent imagery.

Generally, you keep your tone and your behavior but apply it to a new world. You keep your music, and you change your lyrics. You say "yes" without giving up your central way of behaving.

FIGHT WELL

Fights are tricky in improv. Quick disagreements, long debates, and screaming matches are all potential sand traps that will catch your scenes and drag them under. Fights are so tricky that teachers generally tell beginners to avoid them completely. "Don't fight" is a frequent note in early levels, but that's too severe. We need to fight in scenes; we just have to learn how to fight well.

Improv rules change when you're in a fight. Suddenly to "yes and" you must be disagreeable, as a character, and do the opposite of what your scene partner asks. Suddenly you need to deliberately play a bit below the top of your intelligence and argue for a point you know is foolish.

Your animal instincts will really screw you when a fight starts. You'll make brilliant and rational excuses for your behavior, when really the scene needs you to shamelessly do more of whatever you were accused of. Time will fly when you're in a fight. You won't even notice that the scene has frozen.

Actors who have very little comedy experience are real suckers for fights. They dig their heels in and will not budge. They are so happy to have a clear desire: to win the fight. There are many performers who can't even imagine a scenario where their character is wrong, much less how funny that might be.

Comedians who are poor actors come around a little faster. They're quicker to grasp that they need to enjoy arguing a foolish point. They enjoy being on the "wrong" side.

A fight done well is a fun dance. Picture two people running together, side by side, and then one of them suddenly decides to turn around and run backwards. Now one of them is facing the wrong direction, but they're both still running together.

Like a lot of things, once you get it, it's easy. You just have to learn to avoid digging your heels in, to be ready to be wrong, and to keep yes-anding even when the only thing on the table is an accusation against you.

DON'T = DO

As I've mentioned, here's a very loose rule of thumb: if a character point-edly tells you not to do something in improv, chances are you should do more of it.

Let's say someone says to you, "I hate how you never clean your room." In the heat of the moment, your desire to play to the top of your intelligence, and to be chill and agreeable, will make you want to say, "I'm sorry! I'll clean it right now." But that's not what they want. They want you to be someone who never cleans their room. Weirdly, being a nice person in the face of an accusation is a denial.

"Don't touch that button" means *touch that button immediately.*

I saw a great scene that had this improbable and fantastic beginning between three players named Curtis Gwinn, John Gemberling, and Brett Gelman.

Curtis: Hey, little buddy, what's wrong?

Gemberling: I'm hooked on gas!

A member of the backline (Andy Rocco) entered the scene with a helium gas canister, blew up a balloon, and then left the gas canister. Gemberling noticed the canister, and his eyes lit up.

Curtis: You better not hit that gas! Here, I'm going to put on these sunglasses and earphones and turn the other way while I read this magazine.

Gemberling approached the canister. Then this happened:

Brett Gelman: *(as the canister)* Hey, little boy...

Gemberling: Wait a second! Gas canisters don't speak English!

Brett Gelman: *(haltingly)* El pequeño muchacho, ¿viene toma una canistero de gasia?

Then, Gemberling took a big hit of helium gas. Huge laughs.

This whole scene was built around someone being forbidden to do something, and then doing it anyway. Doing what you are told not to do is saying yes, and often extremely fun.

MAKE THE ACCUSATION TRUE

The main way that fights fail in a scene is that people stop yes-anding each other. We stop learning anything about the characters and the world. Everything stops while the people butt heads.

A second loose rule of thumb to follow within fights is to get in the habit of yes-anding accusations, which means making the accusations true.

Your ears should get sensitive to when your character is being accused of something, and you should immediately want to make it true. Sometimes just overtly agreeing with the accusation is the best move.

Player A: Honey, Bob says he saw you out at a restaurant with your aerobics trainer. *(accusation)*

Player B: Yes, I am having an affair with my aerobics instructor. *(agreeing with the accusation, or taking the "wrong" side)*

A: You admit to having an affair?

B: Yes.

A: Why would you do this to me?

B: Because I'm committed to getting good at aerobics! *(justification thought of at that time)*

Now we're learning more about the characters. We're moving forward and building on what has happened. We have more to unpack and play with going forward.

Think of accusations as a casting breakdown. When someone says, "Well, you're the one who had the affair." Don't think, "How can I explain myself?" Instead think, "I've been cast as someone who cheats on his spouse."

REJECT SOLUTIONS

A common trap is creating a problem and then trying to solve it. Solving problems is being stuck in the future. *Maybe we should do this? How about this?* Instead, reject the solution and make the problem worse.

Here's a scene between performers Max Sosna-Spear and James Mannion, about a guy who has become obsessed with the movie *Kramer vs. Kramer*, a very serious 1979 dramatic film about a couple getting divorced.

> **Max:** Adrian, every one of your DVD boxes has *Kramer vs. Kramer* in it.

> **James:** Yeah, well my parents got divorced like a week ago, and it's really the only movie left that I've been able to relate to.

> **Max:** You got all of these copies of *Kramer vs. Kramer* in the last week?

> **James:** Yeah! Well, I had to do something! I couldn't do anything else except think about it!

> **Max:** Oh, geez, I'm so sorry.

> **James:** I just kept going on eBay, ordering another one and another one.

> **Max:** That's sad. I'm so sorry. Do you want me to help you put all the right DVDs back in the cases?

Max is playing truthfully, so he offers a reasonable solution. That's fine because it keeps the scene feeling truthful, but James rightly rejects the solution in order to protect the unusual thing.

> **James:** I don't want to watch any of that other garbage! The other stuff is made up! It's not real! Look at this: *Die Hard!* This is just an escapist fantasy! *Kramer vs. Kramer* is the only movie with any sort of reality to it!

A reliably fun reaction to anyone offering to solve the problem is to do more of the problem. James could have said:

> **James:** I don't want to put the regular DVDs back! In fact, I'm going to put two copies of *Kramer vs. Kramer* in each of these cases, so I have backups.

Or you can do a "bait and switch," where you appear to accept the solution but then reject it.

> **James:** Yeah, that's a good idea. Let's get the regular DVDs back in these cases. *Kramer vs. Kramer* is coming out on Blu-ray, so I'm going to have to buy it in that version anyway.

Reject solutions that try to get rid of the unusual thing.

ARGUE THAT THE WORLD IS FLAT

A common strategy to make fights funny is to argue the dumb side of any discussion. Take the wrong side and defend it as best you can.

Let's call this arguing that the world is flat. Imagine two characters are arguing whether the world is flat or round. The position that the world is flat is obviously more fun.

Any time you find yourself in a fight, make sure that at least one or possibly both of you are arguing something surprising, or wrong, or even a little dumb.

Here's a scene from improv group Convoy, off the suggestion "dishwasher." Alex Berg plays a guy who insists that a dishwasher cannot handle washing a colander. Todd Fasen plays a normal human.

> **Fasen:** It's broken, I don't know.

> **Berg:** Well, we shouldn't have put the colander in it.

> **Fasen:** No, the colander's not going to ruin the dishwasher.

> **Berg:** It's not a dish!

> **Fasen:** What?

Berg: A colander's not a dish!

Fasen: You put silverware in there, and silverware's not a dish either! Stop scapegoating the colander for all these problems!

Berg: I'm just saying it's such hubris putting a colander in there. You hand-wash a colander! Everyone knows that!

Fasen: No, you can put a colander in the dishwasher. You want to hand-wash pots and pans. I think most things you could put in a dishwasher.

Berg: I agree with you on pots and pans. It's on the colander where we just don't see eye to eye!

Fasen: Look, I think it's the fact that you bought a dishwasher at a garage sale for us!

Berg: Hey, I got a good deal!

Fasen: It can't handle most things!

Berg: It's not MEANT to handle a colander! It's meant to handle a dish!

Fasen: I think a dish is more hearty than a colander!

Berg: No, no, no! A colander has all the holes in it, it mish-mashes the water every which way!

Then Alex Fernie tags them out and begins a business meeting. Berg and Fasen become his co-workers.

Fernie: Gentlemen, the fourth-quarter numbers are not good. They're 33% below our projections. The only thing I can think to blame is the colander.

Berg: Hey, we factored the colander into our projections!

Fernie: Well, the numbers are terrible. And I look around here and I have to notice, well, why is a colander working for a company?

Berg: It came with great recommendations. Personal references were through the roof. It can't be the colander. I blame Jones. *(pointing to Fasen)*

Fasen: I think we're giving too much responsibility to the colander. We're the top video game company in North America, and we told the colander to design our new video game.

Fernie: This isn't the time to point fingers. What we need right now...

Fasen: I'm pointing a finger at the colander!

Berg: I pointed one at Jones!

Fernie: Look, we have to figure out something to do. We're looking at another year in the red and we're gonna go under, colander or not.

Berg: I agree. What if we let the colander run the marketing campaign for Uncharted 4?

Berg uses as intelligent an argument as he can muster to defend himself throughout, citing personal references and recommendations. In that last line he rejects a reasonable solution in favor of doubling down on trusting the colander.

None of this breaks the "play to the top of your intelligence" guideline, because you will argue the dumb thing as smartly as possible. That's practically the definition of a joke: argue a dumb thing in a smart way.

SYMPATHETIC DISAGREEMENT

A good technique to use during an improv argument is "sympathetic disagreement." This refers to tone.

A character says something, and your character disagrees. But while disagreeing, your character says he or she understands why the other person feels that way.

In other words: yes-and the accusation, even as you disagree with it. Something like, "Look, I get it, but...."

You say: "Hey, I bought a hamburger at this Wendy's, and there is a full finger in it!" The responder, accepting the accusation and making it true, says: "Our chefs are the best. I assume this finger was put in there on purpose and is going to be delicious."

They are handling a gift you made up, so it's bad form to attack them too aggressively here. It's a bit hard to think when someone is yelling at you, even when it's a make-believe character. Using some sympathetic disagreement allows you to keep your opinion while giving them some breathing room.

You say: "Hey, I'm all for trying new delicacies, okay? I didn't think I'd like Thai food; turns out I love Thai food. But I'm sure that a finger is not a delicacy."

Emotion is good in general, but within a fight too much anger distorts things. People get defensive and stop adding any information. Sympathetic disagreement lets you keep your honest reaction without digging in your heels too much.

EXERCISES FOR FIGHTING IN SCENES

EXERCISE:
SUPERVILLAIN / MASTERMIND

Two people up. Player A makes an accusation. Player B deliberately acts like a supervillain or mastermind in response. Player A must then sympathetically disagree (otherwise, Player A will often get too angry).

> **Player A:** Jeremy, did you use all the conditioner?

> **Player B:** Bwa ha ha, yes, I did! Now your hair will look stringy and flawed! And I shall look more beautiful by comparison!

> **Player A:** *(sympathetically disagreeing)* Look, I know that I can be arrogant about my hair, but this is really going too far.

PROS: Player B practices being the "bad" character while still taking full ownership of the accusation. The sympathetic disagreement prevents Player A from attacking too aggressively. It lets Player B catch their breath and fully digest this position they have been gifted. The exercise is silly and entertaining and fun. It's clear and easy to measure if you've done it right.

CONS: Resulting scenes are kind of dumb.

OWN IT

Same thing, but now Player B must admit to the accusation and explain why as a "normal" person, not a supervillain. Player A still sympathetically disagrees.

> **Player A:** Jeremy, did you forget to invite anyone to this party?

> **Player B:** I did it on purpose. I wanted the party to fail, because I'm jealous of you having friends besides me.

> **Player A:** Yes, I know I've been ignoring you, but you're acting like a child!

PROS: As an exercise, it's still easy to follow. It makes Player B use the accusation as a way of learning more about his or her character. In an improv scene, this strategy will actually work very often.

CONS: Although more natural than the supervillain one, this one can still feel forced and contrived, and the scenes all take on a similar feel.

A REAL REASON

Same set up, but this time Player B tries to feel why they would have done such a thing for real. Like, in real life. The only condition here is that you have to accept without argument that you really have done the thing: you can't change it so you didn't do it, or say that you didn't do it on purpose.

For example, if Player A says, "Sir, we found these knives and excessive liquids in your luggage. Why were you sneaking these onto the plane?"

If you were doing supervillain approach, you might say, "So I can take over the skies!"

If you were doing the "own it" approach, you might say, "Because I plan on using them to bully other passengers up there."

I actually think both of those responses could work. But if you take a moment and try to feel why you might really have done it, I bet you'd take a moment to consider, and then say something like this:

"You know, I was just hoping you wouldn't check. I thought I could get away with it. I think the TSA policies are kinda dumb. I'm not planning anything bad, and I just didn't care to follow your rules."

PROS: The answers are rich, specific, and have the ring of truth that makes improv compelling. This is what the best improvisers often do when endowed with a strange situation. It is the best approach in actual scenes.

CONS: It's hard to measure, from the student's perspective, if you've done this right. Students don't necessarily know what truth feels like on stage. And since there are so few restrictions on how you respond, many students will inadvertently deflect: "I don't know! Someone else must have put them there!" or "Ach, I took the wrong bag by mistake!"

The exercise basically says "be good actors and be interesting people," which is not the most helpful instruction, but this is the best approach in a scene. Give a "real" answer.

BE BRAVE

For many improvisers, there's nothing scarier than an accent. Someone starts a scene in a British accent, and the other improviser suddenly goes into mental overdrive trying to figure out how he can explain why he doesn't have to have a British accent also.

For others, there's nothing more jarring than playing a different gender. You're a woman who gets labeled as a man, and you'd rather just play a woman, so you create some huge backstory to explain why this person thought you were a man, but no, really, you're a woman.

For others, there's nothing more intimidating than a serious and dramatic topic. Someone tells you that your character has cancer, and you inwardly dread the rest of the scene. "How can I be funny now that you brought cancer up?" The idea of just responding honestly seems terrifyingly boring.

For others, there's nothing more nerve-wracking than being the one to answer the big question. Everyone is saying they are scared of some guy named Dave, and making a big deal about it, and you don't want to be the one to make the big choice about why you're all scared of Dave, because you don't want to be "wrong."

For others, there's nothing more unsettling than sitting a scene out, even though it's going fine and doesn't need anyone else.

Improv has a way of making you do whatever you're scared of as an actor. You hate nothing more than dancing? The audience will give you the suggestion "Dirty Dancing." You hate being a talking animal? Your scene partner is going to make you an emu, and you don't even know what that is. If you never watch television, then your scene is going to be one where you have to imitate the star of the new hit show "Happy Mondays," which the audience all knows and loves.

You can avoid all of these things if you're quick-witted enough to dodge them, but it's often better to do the thing you're scared of. "Follow the fear," as the saying goes.

A note I got in an early improv class was: "Will, you're just watching the scene. You need to be *in* it." This was from John Cameron Telfer, a teacher at Chicago City Limits. It was one of those notes I knew I needed for my real life as well as the scene I was in. I was avoiding really feeling things as they were happening.

Years later, in an Upright Citizens Brigade practice, I was in a scene featuring everyone as miners trying to break into a collapsed mine. I chose to be a photographer, staying on the outside, snapping photos. My coach, James Eason, shouted: "Will: PARTICIPATE!" *My old habit,* I thought. I dropped my camera and got to my knees to join the other miners.

The right choice is often the brave choice. The character from the opening that you're scared of doing. The opinion you're worried the audience won't agree with. The object work you think no one will understand. You just have to commit and do it. Visualize your spine made of flexible steel and jump into it.

The audience will love it. Improv is more about confidence than it is accuracy. Maybe it's straightforward: brave things are also difficult or surprising things, and therefore more enjoyable for the audience. Or maybe the audience can smell the bravery on you, and they become fascinated.

Once, at UCB in New York, Amy Poehler asked to meet with all the teachers to give us her thoughts on teaching improv. We were all thrilled to meet with one of our comedy heroes. We didn't have a classroom big enough to hold all the teachers, so we went up a floor from our school to an unfurnished floor above us. Amy sat in the lone folding chair, and all the other teachers stood around her in this big cavernous space.

One of Amy's most emphatic pieces of advice was not to let students quit in scenes. They don't have to be funny or good in early classes, she said, but right from the first day of level one, we can't let them quit. No bailing. Nip that in the bud, she said.

Staying in your scenes even when you're not sure what to do next is the kind of bravery we need. It makes the scenes exciting.

Bravery means "making brave acting choices" and does not mean "putting up with intrusive choices that make you feel gross." You don't have to be picked up, or be physically pushed around, or talk about sexual or violent topics if you don't want to. See "You Don't Have To Be Picked Up" under the "Difficult People" section.

What I'm talking about is acting. You know it when you're playing scared. Be brave.

KNOW, CARE, SAY

You've heard these rules of improv:

- "Don't ask questions."
- "Avoid teaching or transaction scenes."
- "Don't be coy."
- "Know your scene partner."
- "Be affected."

You know them. Every improv theater community has these rules and a handful of others in the same vein.

All of those rules, in all of those variations, boil down to this:

In your improv scenes, characters should generally:

- KNOW what they're doing,
- CARE about whatever the main issues of the scene happen to be, and
- SAY how they feel about things.

It is not intuitive to behave this way. We are socialized against doing all of this.

In real life we tend to openly declare when we don't know, and apologize. We ask questions.

We walk away from situations that we don't care about. We don't react to things that are crazy or weird.

We keep our mouth shut all the time to avoid problems. We don't speak.

These are your first acts of bravery: choosing to know, care, and say. By doing them, you are overcoming socialized habits and keeping your scenes interesting.

Know

Try not to say, "I've never done this before!" or "This is my first day!" or "The boss isn't here!" or "This wasn't my decision." Instead, say, "I know what to do," and "I AM the manager here." It's okay if you don't really know about the specifics of a given situation; just play the emotional truth. You may not know anything about car engines, but if you are a car mechanic in a scene, you know generally the way a person talks when describing what's wrong with a car.

Care

Saying "I don't care" is boring. If your boss fires you, give a shit. Being bored or unaffected kills scenes, and is usually done by an actor not skilled enough to adjust to something that surprised them.

Find reasons to get passionate about the topic at hand. Here's a scene in which, off the suggestion "brutal," one actor (Colin McGurk) reacts to the other (Christopher Corbin) having just passed horrific gas.

Colin: Oh, God! Chris, what do you eat, man?

Christopher: I had a lot of cauliflower and brussels sprouts today. I'm on a veggie raw diet.

Colin: I gotta work in here! We work in this environment together!

Christopher: I know, man, but I feel awkward because I don't want to go into the next room because Jeanene's in there. Feel like it's better in front of a guy.

Colin: Okay, all right. I guess that's a code I can follow.

They have opinions they feel strongly about, and they find a way to feel even more strongly about them.

Christopher: My tummy is doing circles. My wife is getting on me about my weight.

Colin: Your wife? Why are you nervous about Jeanene, then?

Christopher: Because she's a woman. My mom raised me to not fart in front of women!

Colin: I didn't know that! You're MARRIED? I thought you were just nervous because you had a thing for Jeanene or something. You have a wife? GO FART IN FRONT OF A WOMAN RIGHT NOW!

Christopher: I WILL NOT!

Colin: It's not that big a deal to fart in front of a woman!

Christopher: I was brought up right! And I'm gonna stay that way!

It's Christopher's passion, his deep caring, that makes his opinion so funny.

Say

Here's a scene where Frank Banz confesses to a baseball player he's coaching, played by Seth Gilbert, that he has the player's father's heart inside of him.

Frank: Chandler, I just want to say... that was a really good triple you hit out there.

Seth: Thanks.

Frank: I've got your father's heart.

Seth: What?

Frank: Your father died. And I was his batting coach. And I have your father's heart. And I want you to know when you hit that triple today, it made me cry. And I feel that part of him is in me. Because normally I'm happy for people when they make a hit but, man, I got all teared up.

Seth: I don't even have a response to that. It's like, he died like two years ago, so two years ago when we were working together and you took that vacation that... I'm speechless!

Frank: Who doesn't take vacation?

Seth: But how did you plan it?

Frank: I've always had a bad heart. I planned it. We planned it.

Seth: You and my father were in collusion to work this out together?

Frank: Yes. He said if I ever die, I'm donating mine to you.

Seth: Why did you choose this moment? This is the beginning of...?

Frank: Because I almost cried and I looked like an idiot out there. If I see you hit again, I'm just leaving the stadium!

Seth: This is the World Series, game 7. This is it! If I don't go up...

Frank: *(crying)* My little boy!

The rules are trying to get you to know, care, and say. In fact, once you automatically start to do that in scenes, you can forget the rules. We often say to "avoid transaction scenes," but once you're experienced you can do a transaction scene, because you're doing one in which you know the person, you care about what you're buying, and you say what you think about it.

"FIND THE LOVE"

Being brave as I'm describing it has to do largely with acting. A good note on acting comes from longtime casting director Michael Shurtleff's book *Audition.*

The advice is "find the love."

Shurtleff says that no matter how dry the audition piece seems, you can find the love between the characters. Even if it's angry, that anger comes from love. It's on the actor to find it.

This applies to the start of improv scenes. No matter what the situation, find a reason to care about what's going on in it.

"I COME TO AN IMPROV SHOW TO BE BLOWN AWAY."

Besides knowing, caring, and saying, bravery in an improv scene is also a group-wide decision to make cool stuff happen.

Here's a scene I saw when I was a student: two people were a couple in a casino about to play roulette, and they argued a bit before settling on number 27. The scene wasn't going great, but they pressed on. No one even stepped out to be the croupier. Someone on the back line did a half-hearted sound of a ball clicking around a roulette wheel. And then the sound stopped, and someone else on the back line made this decision:

They said, "27."

The couple won! They got really excited and started thinking of how they would spend the money. Maybe we'll get a big dinner, they said, or upgrade our room at the hotel. Then the wife said, "Let's bet again. Same number." They put it all on 27.

The guy who made the sound of the clicking before did it again. Then the guy who was the croupier once again said, "27."

The couple went more nuts. They jumped and hugged. They started talking about how they might buy a car. Or maybe take a trip to the Bahamas. They were specific and funny about their wishes. Then the husband said, "Again." And they bet it all on 27.

Click-click-click. "27."

The couple went absolutely apeshit. They screamed, "I love you!" to each other! They said they're gonna go around the world! They're going to get a bag of cocaine and do it all even though they've never done drugs! They're gonna make a baby! They're gonna bet one more time!

Click-click-click. "27."

The couple screamed! The class loved it. Then the teacher, Ali Farahnakian, edited the scene and said, "Kudos for the decision to make them keep winning. That's what I want. *I come to improv shows hoping to be blown away.*"

The lesson was clear. Top of your intelligence would say you can't win that many times in a row. But a good sense of theatrics and patterns says: yes, it can happen.

You can't just jump straight to such huge outcomes. You have to earn it step by step. You can't break reality, but you should, with good comedic taste, bend it. See the section "Take the Local" under "Be Authentic."

DON'T MAKE IT ABOUT MONEY

Money is a big part of life, but a boring part of improv scenes. When you let scenes become about money, you're usually dodging the funny part and avoiding the trickier problem of engaging with an unusual philosophy. Be brave and engage.

DON'T LET THE STRAIGHT MEN WIN

There are two kinds of bad improv shows: too silly and too careful.

Too silly is the worst, certainly. These are the ones where everyone is playing very broadly, bugging their eyes out and walking in huge exaggerated strides, practically turning to the audience with every line and making a face. Every character gets ratcheted up to the most farcical version. Every spouse is cheating, every boss is mean, every employee is stealing money. No one has internal motivations, just knee-jerk worst case scenarios. It's as if the actors are trying to entertain children. These types of shows are bad for improv and comedy and America.

In these shows, empty silliness is winning, and commitment is losing.

But a real close second for "worst kind of improv show" is the show that is too careful. Usually done by students who have had a few classes and have been scolded to "play to the top of your intelligence" and to "treat your fellow players like poets and geniuses," these shows feature people talking too softly to be heard, sitting in chairs, and refusing to feel any emotions about anything at all, as they fold their arms and quibble the scenes into permanent boredom. Worst of all, no one makes any choices.

Everyone is so reasonable and careful and real and critical and hesitant that the show sucks.

In those shows, the straight men are winning, and fun is losing.

It feels like fear is keeping people in their seats. Fear of making a wrong move, fear of looking dumb, fear of breaking some rule you can barely remember. You need to get over fear and play characters who are active, make choices, provoke action, and show reaction.

Now, sure, you want voices of reason in your show. We often need characters who notice what is strange, and who are affected and confused by the funniness of the scene.

They should never get the upper hand, though. We shouldn't spend too much time with them, and they should "lose" the scene.

YOU DO NOT HAVE TO BE PICKED UP

Here's a very important caveat to being brave: you never have to do anything on stage that makes you feel uncomfortable. This is different than being brave. Being brave is about being a brave actor: willing to do accents, be emotionally vulnerable, make the big choice, etc.

But what if someone gets too physical or intrusive? Or keeps pushing opinions onto your character that you just don't want? Do you have to "say yes" and "accept the offer" and go along with that?

Fuck no! Push back, and say no. Physical intrusiveness is rude, and no one wants it.

I'm talking about stuff that is blatantly wrong, like getting handsy, trying to kiss someone, or dirty dancing. You can say no, push back, and get some space. The teacher or coach should notice this category of rudeness.

This also includes stuff that some people are cool with. What if someone is yelling too close to your face? Or tries to physically pick you up? Some people don't mind being picked up, but lots of people do. You are allowed to set your own boundaries and push back.

You'll want to check with yourself that you're not just being scared of an acting choice. Someone asking you to be a character who simply talks about sex is probably not being intrusive. Someone who is insisting on giving you a lap dance is.

Here's how you handle it. Often a quick "no" in character is enough.

Player A: Honey, it's time for our anniversary lap dance!

Player B: Ew! No. Cut that out.

If they try to endow you with an opinion you don't want, you can just say you've changed your mind. Saying why is good form here.

Player A: No lap dance? But you always love lap dances.

Player B: I have in the past. I have enjoyed your lap dances. But now I'm realizing... I think it might be really gross and weird.

See "You Already Know The Real Why" under "Be Authentic," for more on picking truthful explanations for your behavior.

Everyone's boundaries are different. Some people might not mind a lap dance in a scene. Your boundaries may change from year to year, from team to team. You are allowed to decide. Push back confidently and easily with no guilt. You can change your mind even later in the same scene if you want.

Improv is about being a brave actor, yes. But it's never about being actually uncomfortable. You are a co-writer of every scene you're in. You're allowed to say no and push back always.

BE BRAVE EXERCISES

A good shortcut to knowing, caring, and saying is to make the scene about the people in the scene.

A common error for newer improvisers is when two characters spend the whole scene talking about a third character who isn't there. The spouse, the boss, the crazy friend. It feels natural, but a scene can't really get started until the people in it talk to each other *about each other.*

In real life, we rarely talk to each other about each other. We're scared to do it, or it feels rude.

But for our improv scenes, we have to get comfortable speaking directly.

A good exercise to practice this is to do two-person scenes in which each person must start their lines with "I," "you," or "we." Do this until you feel the scene has found a game.

Making a scene about the characters we can see generally makes the scene more powerful.

Here's a scene between Chris Kula and Billy Merritt.

Chris enters as a customer in line at a counter, looking up over a cashier at a menu.

Billy enters to be the cashier. He adopts a stern face and stares intently at Chris.

Chris: Hmmm, I'm not sure what to get.

Billy: Look at me.

Chris: What? No, I...

> **Billy:** Don't look up there. Look at me. I will help you. Look right at me.

That subtle bit, just saying "look right at me," was enough to get the audience laughing. Now the actors still had work to do to determine what the scene was about.

> **Chris:** No, I just am not sure what…

> **Billy:** You want to see *The Revenant?*

The Revenant was a real movie out at the time.

> **Chris:** I'm not sure. I saw an ad for it and it didn't really grab me.

> **Billy:** All we have here is *The Revenant.* I got rid of the other movies.

The game of this scene is a movie theater that has only one movie. But Billy's "look at me" gave the whole scene a menacing tone, and gave them something to unpack about a person in the scene right away.

Do two-person scenes in which each character makes a confession to the other one at some point. "I have something to admit to you." That kind of confession. Confessions are a good way to jump-start a stalled scene, because they make you say something personal, honest, and important.

They also tend to make the scene very much about the characters in it.

Here's a scene between Lisa Timmons and Raymond Lew.

> **Ray:** I've been working so much on a PowerPoint presentation for Nathan. It's... it's just insane.

> **Lisa:** That's why you've been too busy for everything else? *(She gestures at their chess board.)* This "Nathan," he rules you.

> **Ray:** He's the CEO of the company! I'm taking time out of my day to meet you here in Palisades Park, all right? I expect a little more compassion.

> **Lisa:** All right.

> **Ray:** Seems like you don't even want to play now.

> **Lisa:** I'm letting you win!

> **Ray:** I appreciate that, but... well, I would feel better if I didn't feel obligated to play chess.

The scene needs a boost. A confession from Lisa rights the ship.

> **Lisa:** I have a confession to make. This Nathan? I hired him. To distract you from your game.

There's a big laugh, and Ray suddenly has a lot to unpack.

> **Ray:** No! He has a corner office! He's been on CNN, talking to *Mad Money!* How can you... just... make him up?

> **Lisa:** I am very rich.

The confession focused the scene to be about the characters we are watching.

This is an exercise that is simple to explain, though a bit tricky to do.

Do scenes where the goal is to blow the audience away.

In the spirit of the roulette example, do a series of scenes where you are trying to blow the audience away with how far things go.

Make more interesting choices with greater commitment than you normally think you're allowed to. Feel your power. (Don't be physically intrusive.)

Sometimes it's good to have an exercise that is simply a big challenge. Rather than a strict structure, it's on you to make this happen. *Find a way to blow the audience away.* You'll have to get creative. You might want to start slowly, giving yourself room to find new possibilities.

FOLLOW THE FOLLOWER /
SOUND AND MOVEMENT

"Sound and movement" is a kind of opening. It is notoriously weird and annoying, and is one of those things that seems so useless at first that it will make you doubt whether you should be doing improv at all.

However, there are also great lessons to be learned in it—about letting go and letting the animal part of your brain make decisions before your inner judge screws it all up. About hearing and reacting intuitively, versus struggling to figure out a logical move.

Doing a sound and movement and then immediately doing scenes will bring out a confidence in many players that they previously did not have. It will get people out of their heads. It will make them play more physically and less hesitantly. It's a great thing to do as an exercise to practice playing more boldly.

"Sound and movement" is a version of "follow the follower," so let's explain that first.

Follow the Follower
In "follow the follower," the whole group stands in a circle and starts in a neutral position. Then the teacher says go. Everyone should start copying and heightening each other, meaning: whatever you see someone else doing, you start doing, but more.

At first, because everyone starts in a neutral position, you will just be copying very gentle sways and twitches. Then you will amplify those sways a bit—into a more pronounced, exaggerated version. Then people will copy the way you are swaying, but they'll do it even more.

No one leads. You just copy. Any time you see two or three people doing something, you just start doing it, only more. No thinking, just doing. If anyone makes even the slightest sound or even breathes in a noticeable way, you copy that.

There is a group-wide agreement that you will let the action change and morph easily. Don't get stuck doing any one thing for too long.

You can make non-verbal noises, meaning no actual words. Commit, meaning you do the physical gestures with full enthusiasm, as opposed to shyly doing them just a little bit. The group can break out of the circle if it naturally happens and start wandering around the room like dust particles, all still copying each other.

Do this for 3–5 minutes.

In general, exercises of follow the follower tend to be a bit similar. You will get tired of them if you do too many within a short period, but they are a great warm-up that forces you to get out of your head, pay attention to others, and give up control. They're silly in a way that makes you get over yourself so you can do improv.

By itself, this is a good warm-up to do in a class.

Sound and Movement

Now, a "sound and movement" is like follow the follower, but you start with a suggestion, and there's a bit of structure thrown in.

You get a suggestion, and everyone starts doing a physical activity or motion inspired by the suggestion. Simple and bold is best. If it's "kettle," you all start miming that you're pouring kettles, while making the sound of hot steam pouring out. Everyone copies each other, and, using your "follow the follower" technique, this quickly morphs into an abstracted physical repetition that doesn't really mean anything.

Whatever it is you're doing will morph a few times. You'll be pouring kettles and making steam noises, and then you're just sort of waving your arms up and down in front of you while making some kind of whooping noise, and then you're all skipping around the room, and then you're all jumping up and down saying the word "jump" over and over.

This is where you wonder if you should be doing improv at all. Stay with us, please.

What you're looking for as a group is for your sound and movement to become something recognizable and real. At the point I just described, maybe it almost looks like you're shooting basketballs, so someone just goes ahead and makes their motion into shooting a basketball. Someone else notices and also starts shooting a basketball. And for a few moments you stop doing a "follow the follower" and you're just doing about 20 seconds of shooting basketballs around. You might fill out the scene. Someone goes under a hoop to catch rebounds and throw the ball back in. You pass to each other.

Then, after 20 seconds or so, you go back into "follow the follower" mode and let it become abstract. Things morph and change until you find another recognizable situation.

Think of your sound and movement as having "hallways" and "rooms." The hallways are the abstract portions, where you're just doing follow the follower. The "rooms" are when it temporarily becomes something real.

You do this until you've had 3–4 rooms, and then you try to end on the same activity you started with. Then someone sweeps it and you're done. The whole thing should be 4–5 minutes.

This exercises forces you to stop thinking and to start watching and committing. Get out of your head, watch your scene partners, and make decisions as a group. Yes, your decisions will be simple and big, as opposed to specific and personal—but they'll be fun and bold.

Scenes

Next, you do scenes inspired by your sound and movement.

When I say "inspired by," I simply mean you take any one of the big physical activities and start a scene with it. Maybe you start by shooting a basketball. Or maybe you just start with waving your arms up and down in front of you, but you make it that you're swatting away flies, or something else that could actually happen in the real world.

Obviously you won't be initiating with full ideas, because you're just starting with a physical motion.

The interesting side effect of this is that people will play boldly and decisively. People who are normally timid will be brave and confident. People who have never acted will enter a scene with real swagger.

The sound and movement will have helped everyone get out of their heads. People will jump off the back line to join scenes. People will make decisions confidently and quickly. And yes, the scenes will also be a bit sillier and broader, but it will teach a young group what confidence and physicality feel like.

I don't recommend this for a show, generally speaking. It's too abstract and makes things too silly. Having said that, I was on a team that was having trouble getting along and not committing well in our shows. We started doing sound-and-movement openings for our shows, and they got better. Sure, after a short time the openings got too similar, and we had to move on, but for a burst they did help us play together.

COMPLIMENT/BOAST

This is an exercise to boost the confidence and vulnerability of members of a group.

WARNING: This is a touchy-feely exercise. You have to get over being cool, which is the point.

I recommend this for the last session of an eight-week course, or for teams who are a bit burnt out or in their heads. It is good either at the top of a rehearsal or after a break.

DIRECTIONS
Split up into pairs. If there's an odd number, the teacher should join a pair.

PHASE ONE: Compliments
When the teacher says go, one person in the pair starts complimenting the other on their improv—what they do, the way they do it, anything.

At 45 seconds the teacher says "switch," and now the person who had been getting complimented does the complimenting.

PHASE TWO: Boasting
This is the harder part.

Everyone switches into a new pair. When the teacher says go, one person boasts about their own strengths in improv to the other person. Say what you're good at. Boast about the version of yourself on a good day; it's okay if you don't always do the thing you're bragging about. The person who's listening should help by nodding.

The teacher should tell the class that they are being given permission to boast. Being on stage requires a bit of an ego, so boosting your own before you act is not self-indulgent but necessary. The audience, your team, and you all want the confident version of you on stage, so this boasting exercise is actually helpful to everyone. It is also good to practice bolstering your own view of yourself, as a balance against the negative voice that can get into every performer's head from time to time.

At 45 seconds, the teacher says "switch," and the other member of the pair boasts.

It's not nearly as hard as it sounds, and everyone leaves the class feeling pretty great.

This exercise is also good to force wannabe comedians to stop trying to be smarter and funnier than everyone, and to make them be emotionally vulnerable once in a while.

BACKGROUND

I learned this when I took a monologue study workshop in the fall of 2001. I had been put on a house improv team at the Upright Citizens Brigade shortly before this. It was my first time being a regular performer, and I was terrified of not being up to the task, so I started going to an acting class. It was a drop-in monologue study workshop run by a guy named Rob McCaskill, who'd taught an improv course I'd taken a few years before.

Doing "real" acting was extremely frightening. I was a computer programmer, and everyone else in this monologue drop-in class were these very emotive, actorly actors. The first day, I performed the monologue from the end of *Cool Hand Luke,* feeling silly and scared as I did it.

I liked Rob a lot. He gave generous, pragmatic advice that was easy to do and didn't make me feel terrible. It ranged from very direct things ("Try a longer pause after each period," "Pick a specific person you're addressing") to more general stuff ("Let this get simpler," "Do less"). Just the act of going to this course made me feel braver, and the actual advice also improved my performance.

Rob would often have us start the workshops with this compliment/boast exercise. It reminded me that the other actors didn't see me as someone who wasn't up to the task, but instead as someone who was being brave and going for it. We were all rooting for each other and focusing on what was working.

TOP OF
THE SCENE

A crucial time for being brave as an actor is at the top of a scene. The very start of the scene can be a frantic time up in your head. You're trying to think of a way to use the suggestion or the opening. You're thinking of the notes you got at the end of your last show. You're wondering who's in the audience. You're thinking about the teammate you're feeling protective of / nervous about / irritated by.

Your attention is often divided a million different ways. That's not good for your scene. Imagine if every time you started driving you were simultaneously baking a soufflé in your car.

It's also bad to get too precious about the start of a scene. If you overly craft an initiation or spend too long on the backline, the show can lose momentum. But there are some simple best practices for the first few lines that can help avoid common communication problems.

START CHILL

Generally, start with your characters pretty chill. Yes, they're ready to react and have opinions and be affected, but underneath that, they should be relaxed and naturalistic.

Do this even if the scene begins in a confusing way. If you don't totally know what's going on, just assume that you will soon figure it out and act normal until then.

If someone starts a scene by saying, "Doctor, here's the scalpel," you should not say, "I'm nervous. This is my first day." That's a dead giveaway that you're a new improviser. You follow the "know, care, say" principle and simply start performing surgery.

It's like that 1990s show *Quantum Leap.* In every episode of that show, the main character would leap into the body of a new person. He'd be right in the middle of a situation, and he'd have to figure out from context clues what was going on. He'd never say, "Hey! I just beamed into this body! I have no idea what's going on!" He'd fake it until he figured it out.

LOOK AT EACH OTHER

Remember to look at each other.

Very often improvisers step out for the start of the scene, and they are deep in their heads crafting a line, or they are looking down at the front of the stage, with their brows furrowed, as if they're headed to a job interview—not seeing each other.

This happens to everyone. Just remember to look up.

STARTING WITH OBJECT WORK DOWNSTAGE RIGHT

An uncanny number of scenes start with someone walking out to the downstage right corner (close to the audience) and getting immersed in object work. Chopping some food, making some contraption, fussing with papers.

There's nothing wrong with a non-verbal start to a scene, as long as you make sure you look back over your shoulder for a quick check-in.

But what often happens is the person doing the object work is up in their head, waiting and crafting the "perfect" start, and the person watching from behind feels totally exposed and is panicking in their silence (though they shouldn't be; see the "Be Comfortable With Silence" section of "Be Present").

Then the person doing the object work will start with a slightly hostile, "Uh, are you gonna help me with these dishes?" when all they really mean is, *psst, I'm doing dishes down here.*

And then the other person, who feels exposed and ignored will say, "I *was!* But first I have to deal with all these maps!" Because they wanted the scene to be about maps.

And then the dishes person will start fighting: "Forget your maps! You with your maps! Always with these maps!"

This is a false fight. The characters aren't mad; the actors are panicking because they didn't check in early enough.

If they had just looked at each other once before talking, none of that would have happened. They would have seen each other, calmed down, and started in a non-hostile way. "Sure are a lot of dishes." That's perhaps a bland initiation, but it's better than a false fight.

INITIATION ETIQUETTE

Don't interrupt or finish someone else's initiation. This is very commonly done by eager alpha bulldogs who are new. Whoever moves first should be given focus and a generous amount of time to make their move. The person who responds also gets a lot of time before they have to answer. Avoid the very common practice of talking until you are interrupted.

If the person who steps out takes a long time to start, then you can say something. But new improvisers are panicky. To them a "long time" is half a second. Let's say that person gets three full seconds.

THE INBOUND PASS

Keep the second line simple, especially if the initiation was complicated at all. Your first and second line should be casual, routine, and problem-free—like an inbound pass in basketball.

In basketball, you start a play by standing just out of bounds, holding the ball. One of your teammates waits on the court. You throw the ball to him; you "inbound" it. Someone from the opposing team is there, too, and they might block your throw a bit, but generally they don't try too hard. The inbound pass is usually no big deal. The real play will happen once the ball is brought up the court a bit.

That's how your scenes should start. Someone initiates in a simple, clear way, and someone responds. Don't make it complicated when you toss it inbound, and don't do anything complicated when you catch it.

When someone says, "Bill, step into my office," you just go, "Sure, what's up?" You don't say, "IS THIS ABOUT HOW I FLOODED THE LOBBY?" That's too much. That'd be like catching the inbound pass and immediately heaving it down the court.

If the first line is confusing for whatever reason, just play it casual and slow. Don't panic.

If someone says something that's sort of inscrutable like, "Citizen, your plate is missing," and there's no real way to know what's going on, still play it nice and casual. Follow the tone of the conversation to fake it until you know what's going on. "My plate is missing? Oh no!"

Here's a scene from improv group Bangarang! between Ryan Stanger and Ryan Meharry. They're inspired by an opening monologist who said that when she was bullied on playgrounds in elementary school the teachers would never get involved.

Notice how much normal conversation they have before Stanger reveals his unusual thing, and that Meharry patiently waits.

Stanger: Hey, I'm gonna lay something on ya. First of all, how are ya? Ya good?

Meharry: Yeah, I'm pretty great.

Stanger: First day of school is always weird. I know you're teaching sixth graders now, and you were doing fifth grade last year. It's not that much of a difference, but sixth grade is its own animal.

Meharry: Yeah, man.

Stanger: So anyway, I feel like you and I connect as teachers.

Meharry: Yeah, I feel like we're both two of the more regular guys here.

Stanger: Totally! We get each other. And so my angle this year is: when people are scrapping out in the playground, and I'm on yard duty, I'm hanging back. I'm not going to involve myself.

Meharry: You're going to let kids fight?

Stanger: I'm gonna let them fight it out! And if somebody gets hurt, somebody... dies... I don't think that's gonna happen, I think they're kinda weak, you know, but if that happens I feel like that's kinda what nature wanted to do, and...

Meharry: I gotta tell you, man, I think that's a really bad idea!

Stanger: I thought you were going to be on board with me on this one!

Meharry: Why would I be on board? You might lose your job over this!

Meharry could sense that Stanger had something, and so he just said "yes" to the facts, waiting for the shoe to drop.

YIN AND YANG

Another way to think about the top of the scene is with the Taoist principles of yin and yang.

Yin is passive, patient, empathetic, malleable. It is akin to a "yes."

Yang is active, assertive, decisive, altering. It is akin to an "and."

After a series of small moves that simply confirm information without adding a lot, it's time for a "yang" move: make a decision, add some information.

But once someone makes a big "yang" move, then it's time for a simple "yin" response. Confirm and unpack what was just added. Even a beat of silence is a good idea.

A scene can handle a few "yin" moves in a row, but too many "yang" moves piled on top of each other clogs the scene.

In the previous scene, Meharry heard Stanger say, "I'm gonna lay something on ya," which means a "yang" move is coming. Meharry knew to make simple, confirming "yin" moves until he heard Stanger drop the bomb.

DON'T BE ALLERGIC TO THE WORLD

The pressure to be funny can be enormous. If you combine this pressure with the confusion that can happen at the top of a scene, you'll end up making the common mistake of being freaked out by the world you're in.

Let's say someone initiates, "Okay, to milk this cow you want to tug on this udder nice and good." That's meant to be a normal, simple beginning, but you're nervous and want something to happen so you seize on some small detail like, "TUG it? You want me to TUG it? Is that really how you milk a cow?"

This happens a lot, especially by people who have been doing a lot of stand-up comedy. They want to make a mountain out of a small detail. That might be the way to go eventually, but not at the top. Just be in the world.

It's especially tempting to be allergic to the world if someone starts a scene that is challenging acting-wise. If someone starts with an accent, or by singing or dancing, or with some very bold physical choice, you'll want to make that the focus of the scene, at least partly so that you don't have to do it. "It's so weird being in England!" or "Don't dance here—everyone's watching!"

Expect to make some sort of internal adjustment at the top of the scene. Might be small, might be big—but expect to do it, and know that this is no big deal. If you're scared to be an actor and play make believe, you'll hurt the scene.

On the other hand, don't ignore really crazy things. If someone is very strange right at the top, which is also common, then don't ignore it.

If someone starts a scene with, "So, you want to sign up at this gym? At this gym, we fuck the weight off you."

It is okay and probably preferable for your character not to want to do that. Just don't be allergic to the surrounding world—in this case, the idea that you came to a gym and wanted to sign up for a membership. That part you should accept. Don't let your shock at that initiation make you say, "How did I even get here? I don't even like gyms!" You should say, "Um, no thanks. I'm not comfortable with having the weight… fucked… off me."

You don't want to be oversensitive to weird things, but if something is big and bizarre then you should react to it and notice it.

REFERENCES

Often someone will start a scene as Darth Vader, Professor Snape, Katniss Everdeen, or Joan of Arc. What if you have no idea who the person they're referencing is? Or worse, you have some small idea, but not enough to feel confident?

This can be scary, but it happens to everyone, a lot. Learn how to handle and enjoy it.

The first possibility is to try to fake it. It is bad form to immediately bail with, "Uh, I don't know who you are. Remind me?" and even worse to completely undo it with the oddly common, "Honey, I know you wanted to role play, but I don't like this game."

Whoever introduced the references should help their scene partners. Tell them what they need to know. If you introduce yourself as Professor Snape, and you see the other person is confused, then you say, "Ah, Harry Potter.

Young wizard student! Here to learn potions from me, your teacher!"

If you've tried to fake it a bit and you still don't know, then you can ask, in character, what is going on. "I'm sorry, I actually can't remember who you are. Remind me?" Your ignorance will be fun, and it'll become part of the scene.

No one should get too detailed. No one likes improv scenes that become trivia contests.

Also, you should try to keep up with what's going on in the world.

You don't have to know everything, and there will always be something you don't know. But make an effort to stay abreast of what the big movies are and what's going on in the news. If there's a celebrity tabloid story, you will get it as a suggestion, so you might as well try to know what the audience is talking about.

Any time someone brings up something in a scene you have never heard of, go home that night, look it up, and learn about it. There are about 20 things that get brought up again and again. You will learn them.

TOP OF THE SCENE EXERCISES

PRACTICE TOUGH BEGINNINGS

Here are some tough beginnings, acting-wise, to practice. Each of these common starts to scenes has something built in that will distract you, unless you tackle it head on with confidence.

For each of these, the characters must talk about something besides what they're doing.

At the top of the scene you are:

- Playing ping pong or volleyball
- Dancing
- Talking with an accent
- Bowling
- Playing blackjack (one dealing, one playing)
- Shopping for books (name books without making the scene about those books)
- Characters from whichever movie is currently popular
- Romeo and Juliet talking (Shakespeare stuff comes up all the time in improv)
- Someone angrily accusing the other of something
- Something weird and specific and fantastical but not a direct reference to any movie, e.g., two people in a room beneath the earth's surface controlling the weather
- George Washington talking to Thomas Jefferson (or any two historical figures)
- Evil witch and good princess
- Scientist and his robot

DIFFICULT PEOPLE

This section is a little different than most of the rest of this book. Instead of talking about the craft of improv moves you can make on stage, I want to touch on the issues of dealing with people when you're off the stage.

I've had a lot of success in the improv world. I went from being a shy person with no acting experience to a respected performer on some of the top teams at the UCB Theatre, as well as one of its most sought-after teachers.

Because of this I'm often asked for advice on how to be successful in an improv community.

When I look back at what I did right—in addition to some things you'd expect, like practice often, watch good shows, work on the fundamentals—I find one thing you don't hear a lot of talk about: I always played well with difficult people.

You learn more playing with good people than with less-good people. That's true. But being judgmental about what's wrong with your teammate's improv is a bad habit that can grow. Judging everyone on stage also means you're judging yourself in a harsh, unhelpful way. Learning to play with anyone is part of getting good.

This goes for getting along offstage, too, within reason. Improv is not just something that happens on stage. It's a community of people. And improv attracts socially awkward people. You are probably one of them to some degree. I certainly am.

But very early in my development as an improviser, I decided to be the person who could and would play with anyone.

PLAYING WITH "BAD" PEOPLE

At first that just meant playing with people that I didn't think were that great. I'm not saying these people were indeed "bad," but that I felt, in my younger, arrogant days, that they were doing improv wrong.

I was inspired by my teacher Ian Roberts, who always ended each class by doing a scene with a student. Invariably, over the eight-session course, he'd do a scene with someone from the class that I didn't consider that great, and the scene would be incredible. I wanted to be that good.

I tried to make it a point in class to step out and do scenes with anyone, especially if it seemed that others in class were avoiding doing scenes with them.

You get better when you play with people that you don't think are doing it "right." Most people are doing the bare minimum of listening and saying yes to the facts. As long as we have that, a good scene should be possible.

If someone in your group is being problematic on stage, my general advice is: "You go to them." If Ian Roberts can make any scene good, then you should be able to work with this person.

Say you're playing with someone who is very aggressive and won't commit and calls out even the slightest unusual thing, always making their own character smug and right. Just play low status (because this person won't leave comfy high status), and let him make fun of your choices while you have fun justifying.

You: I got us tickets to Hawaii for our honeymoon.

Partner: We've been married for 5 years—you're getting tickets *now*?

You: Yeah. I decided it was time.

Partner: But you've always said you hated Hawaii.

You: I know. I panicked. I screwed up.

Partner: Well, I guess we're going. Did you get us tickets to visit a volcano?

You: Yes, a tour of Mount *(made-up name)*.

Partner: That's not a volcano.

You: *(staying low status)* Oh. Then, no, I didn't get any tickets for a volcano.

Partner: Do you hate me? Is that why you're doing all this so badly?

You: I might. I might hate you. I'm sorry. Luckily you find me adorable.

Partner: I don't.

You: You doooo.

It can work as a show and even be mildly fun. You just have to get over the idea of being right or trying to fix them. Connecting is fun, even with a jerk who wants to hog all the good parts. You may look back some time later and see that the person was not as problematic as you once thought.

THE "THAT GUY" PHENOMENON

An incredibly common phenomenon from young improv teams is that they think their group is being held back by one member. If they could just get rid of that one person, they think, everything would be great.

Even when it's true that a person is having difficulty—and it often is true—getting rid of that person will not necessarily fix the group's problem. As Kevin Dorff, a Second City improviser, once told a friend of mine, "If you get rid of 'the guy' then someone else just becomes 'the guy.'"

If you are a newer improviser, with less than two years of experience, and you feel that all of your team's problems come down to one person, try to wait a few weeks. This impulse frequently passes. At every level of improv, there's very often someone seen as "that guy." Someday you may even be seen as that person. Practice some patience before kicking anyone off. Examine yourself and try thinking about it as, "I'm not yet good enough to play with this person."

If you do decide to kick the person out, be honest with them. Tell them to their face what's going on. If they were very invested in the group, it's common to start a new group with a new name, even if it's got almost everyone else from the previous group.

If you've already done this more than once within the span of a few months, improv might not be for you.

DIFFICULT OFFSTAGE

As I progressed with improv, a second and more unexpected case of "difficult person" came up. I met people who were great onstage, but difficult offstage.

Here's where we get into dicey territory. You absolutely do not have to put up with any kind of bad behavior that you don't want to. We all have our own personal limits of what we accept and don't, and you do not have to be ashamed or embarrassed about refusing to put up with certain kinds of behavior.

On the other hand, if you're going to pursue a creative field like improv, you're going to have to work with people who sometimes have fragile egos, volatile temperaments, or somewhat thin skins. It's very common for people who are magnetic and talented performers to be, to some degree, a pain in the ass.

Some people are nervous wrecks before every show, and some will not be able to tolerate any kind of discussion of the show immediately after it. Some will always blame the audience or always want to change coaches after any show goes worse than expected. Some cannot tolerate being tagged out of a scene early. Some will send huge emails detailing their passionate concerns about the state of the team. Some will show up right before a show, saying that they "just want to have fun" tonight, and then will be absolutely insane, breaking every improv rule in sight.

Those things are not too outrageous. I put up with a lot more than that. Among the most extreme things I put up with from talented performers:

- Someone refused to pay dues for three months, so I just covered them.

- Someone raised his fist at a bar and told me he was going to punch me. I didn't believe him, and we stood there for several minutes until he put his arm down. We did a (good!) show together three days later.

- Someone refused to do a show and instead sat in the green room in a crisis, after getting a note from a coach at a rehearsal earlier that day.

- Someone sent an email to the team about problems we were having, "not addressed to anyone in particular," but then detailing several specific moves done by only one player on the team.

- Someone passed around transcripts of chats he'd had with another team member where we were all criticized. Then that other person passed around his version of those chats, which were different. Both suggested the other get kicked off. No action was taken.

- Someone suggested we "go nuts" in a show, and then wore sunglasses and screamed at the audience and tagged everyone out of scenes while he was in them. A few weeks later he sent an email saying he felt like he was the only one who cared about the team.

- Someone disliked a show so much that they stood on the back line with their back to the audience in protest.

- Someone punched a brick wall, hard, to punish himself for having a bad show.

These are the kinds of things you don't want to deal with. (Although, as I read over this list, the only one that really burns me is that someone didn't pay their share of rehearsal costs. I might feel differently if my teammate had actually punched me).

On the other hand, even though they did difficult things offstage, these people were all incredible performers who the audience loved. They made our shows interesting and funny and sometimes great. Some of these people are now successful television and movie writers and performers. I learned a tremendous amount about performing from being on stage with them.

In addition to the bad behavior I listed above, I also had incredibly fun times with these people, including:

- All-night viewing parties of the joyfully worst movies imaginable.

- Last-minute trips to boxing gyms to watch sparring matches.

- Reiki training sessions.

- A sketch show I was in where some of the people referred to in the above list were the only ones who came to watch, and they corralled drunk people from a nearby bar to fill out the audience, resulting in a terrific show.

- Trips to distant pizzerias to watch an elderly Italian chef make dough by hand.

- A graduation performance from an amateur trapeze class.

- Trying psychedelic mushrooms for the first time, immediately followed by a group outing to watch a Harry Potter movie, followed by several hours at someone's house writing a sitcom pilot.

- Lobbying for sponsorship from a farm that trained miniature horses to lead blind people.

- And countless fascinating conversations and arguments after shows.

I can't cleanly separate the fun from the trouble. For some time, as I was learning, putting up with outrageous behavior felt like the good improv move—to say yes and engage the crazy behavior in order to learn more about myself and the world.

You don't have to put up with anything you don't want to, but if you're going to perform with interesting people, you absolutely will have to deal with some degree of chaos. Having some tolerance for it and even being able to enjoy it are necessary skills.

Playing with difficult people made me feel invincible. There is no one with whom I will not perform. There is almost no crazy behavior offstage that can rattle me. If you're willing to step on stage, listen to me, and say yes to the facts of what I'm saying, I can do the show and it will be fun and probably good.

Difficult experiences will also make you appreciate and value the many talented people who are responsible and no trouble at all, and make you work hard to be one of them.

BE
AUTHENTIC

"Improv rules are life rules."
 —Ian Roberts, Amy Poehler, others.

"You've eaten a bowl of cereal a thousand times; just eat it."
 —Owen Burke on doing object work

Here's a problem with improv: it often looks totally dumb.

You've seen big, hammy shows, where the performers make extremely pronounced faces and clownishly huge movements, and talk in affected voices that don't sound like anything real. Big and broad and loud. Everyone is screaming and acting like idiots. These sets look like children's theatre and are an embarrassment to improv.

Before the Upright Citizens Brigade came to New York City, that big, broad style was the only kind of improv I had ever seen. I was a comedy nerd, so I'd often pick up the paper, go to the arts section, see what was listed under "comedy," and check it out. This was in the mid-1990s.

Sometimes I'd see improv shows. They tended to be short form shows, and they were very jokey, very hammy. There were lots of loud, broad voices. The performers would talk to the audience and essentially admit that what they were doing was silly, which was a relief to us in the audience, because it did look silly.

The shows could be fun. But they weren't cool. That, to me, was improv. Kinda fun, mostly silly and dumb. If I wanted "real" comedy I went to see a stand-up show, or maybe a sketch show.

Then the UCB came to town. What struck me right away about their scenes was that they were talking like normal people. They would start scenes so casually, so naturally. They used each other's real names.

Ian would start a scene by looking at Amy and saying, "Amy, can I talk to you a second?" and Amy would go, "Sure, what's up, Ian?"

That was a revelation. *You can do improv and talk like a... real person?*

Even when the scene got silly, their performance style was largely natural. Ian would say, "Did I overhear you saying to your girlfriends that you're planning on hunting me?" and Amy would say, "Yeah! I thought it would be fun. Spice up the relationship! I'm gonna hunt you down."

Then they'd skip forward in time, to show Ian being hunted by Amy. He's crouched down, trying to hide. She's creeping along with a rifle. Ian begs to be spared, "Please! Don't kill me!" And Amy responds, "I thought you didn't want to be like boring people in the suburbs." Maybe her voice would slowly be morphing into that of a deranged killer—but it'd be specific. There was an internal logic to the madness. There was a specificity to the characters.

Also, they didn't apologize for doing improv. They didn't act like what they were doing was so strange and novel. They didn't bother to explain sweep edits or tag-outs. They just did their show and expected that the audience would follow, which we did.

Improv could be cool. You just had to be cool while you did it.

This chapter is about style and taste. You don't technically have to do improv naturalistically. If a group agrees to play silly and listens to each other, then silly can work.

But there is a huge upside to playing it cool and keeping things real, credible, and natural. Let's call it playing "authentically." Bring your real self into what you do. You can still be brave and have the scene blow people away. In fact, it will blow people away even more.

GROUND IT

Your first job in a scene is to ground it. By "ground it," I mean: know the world you're in, or the general type of situation, and relate to it.

Sometimes when an improv coach says "play more grounded," we mistakenly hear that as "play more natural and realistic." Sometimes that is the note, but not necessarily. Think of "being grounded" as "being connected to the ground." The ground is whatever the world is.

Being grounded means being committed to the world. This makes your scenes feel like authentic worlds being lived in, not just the ideas of worlds being talked about.

Watch the very best improvisers listen to an initiation. They are changing their body language as the first person is speaking. They are adapting themselves to fit the vibe and moment of the world it seems like they're in. They're grounding themselves.

You do this before you worry about almost anything else, and certainly before you worry about making the scene funny.

If it's a cowboy-style genre western, then the "ground" is going to be stylized, and you should be, too. This has nothing to do with what your point of view is.

If someone initiates, in a cowboy drawl, "Well, partner, the way I see it, you've got your interior decoration here all wrong. I reckon the piano oughta be closer to the bar," and you say in a normal, natural voice, "I don't understand why you're worried about feng shui!" you will feel the energy drain out of the scene. You didn't connect to its ground. Instead, adopt an appropriate drawl and say, "Now look here, Tex, you gotta let go of this feng shui nonsense and get to worrying about the gunfight later today."

Grounding is more than just using the right voice and tone. Grounding is also relating. Use an "as if" approach to play unfamiliar scenarios—as if they were situations you do know.

When someone endows you as a person on a quest to find a mythical giant, you can internally relate to that situation by playing it "as if" you were about to start a new job that makes you nervous. You borrow the energy and insecurities you would have going into a new job, so that you can play your quest in a grounded way.

Take this example from the improv group Winslow. They do a show in which they interview audience members for stories. An audience member once talked about a running club he belonged to called "Hash House Harriers," which was as concerned with drinking together as they were with running. He said members called it a "drinking club with a running problem."

After that story, Mary Sasson started this scene:

> **Mary:** Jonathan, can you come here for a second?

Jon Mackey entered as the son.

> **Mary:** I was cleaning up your room, and I found a worn pair of sneakers. Have you been getting high?

Jon starts stretching.

> **Mary:** Jonathan, why are you stretching right now?

> **Jon:** Because, Mom, I'm just stretching! Get off my case!

> **Mary:** When did this start?

> **Jon:** When did what start? When did I start spreading my wings and having some fun?

> **Mary:** Was it at school?

> **Jon:** You know when it started? When I sprouted legs, ma!

> **Mary:** You KNOW your dad has tendonitis. It runs in the family!

Jon: What do you want me to say, Mom? Yeah, I went running. And I went running with a bunch of people. We shared the trail, Mom. I didn't sweep it or anything.

Mary: Why are you doing this? Why can't you just walk like other kids?

Jon: Because, Mom, what's the fun in walking? I mean, for real, it takes... where do I go in my days? I go to work at McDonald's, I go to school. Everything is like three or four miles away. If I'm walking, that takes too long.

Drew Tarver enters, "wheeling" himself in a chair.

Drew: Son!

Jon: What, Dad?

Mary: Talk to your son!

Drew: It took me a while to get up the stairs. Your mom says you're running?

Jon: Yeah, Dad! And who are you to say anything? You ran in the Olympics!

Drew: Yeah, and I blew out both my knees! You're gonna follow after me?

Jon: Yeah, maybe I am! Maybe I'm gonna run until my legs fall off!

Mary: Don't say that! Please don't say that!

Drew: I found these tiny shorts in the laundry chute!

Jon: Give me those!

Jon grabs the shorts from Drew's hands, and Drew lunges after them, falling out of his chair. Jon slinks along the floor, sniffing the shorts like drugs.

Mary: Stop that! Stop that! I'm going to call your grandma!

Jon: Don't call her!

Drew: Call Grandma!

Jon: You know what? Call Grandma. She's probably on the treadmill!

Mary: You shut up!

Drew: Your grandma doesn't run. She's too old!

Jon: You guys think Grandma's some shining star of a person, well, you know what? When I visited her last time, not only was she on a normal treadmill, but she put cinder blocks under the front to make it go uphill a little bit.

Drew: *(to Mary, his wife)* Now we know who the bad influence is! It's my mother!

Mary makes a call. Dan Lippert answers, and talks about running "as if" it were using medical marijuana.

Dan: *(out of breath)* Yes?

Mary: Meemaw, have you been running? Why are you out of breath?

Dan: You don't understand, the doctors said it was good for the eyes.

Jon: Yeah, it's medicinal running! It's legal in this state.

Mary: You shut up! You're in a heap of trouble!

Jon: Yeah, well, I'm leaving!

Drew: No, they're getting rid of the gyms with the green crosses in front of them.

Mary: Meemaw, I'll call you back!

Jon: Look, I don't know why you guys have such a big problem with this...

Mano Agapian enters as a UPS driver.

Mano: *(to Drew)* Treadmill delivery!

Drew: Son of a bitch!

Even though many fantastical things occur in this scene (a mom who is threatened by a pair of sneakers, a father who ruined his legs by running too much), it is guided by behavior from real life. The scene is well-grounded and feels truthful.

PLAYING IT REAL: PING PONG TABLE METAPHOR

Think about an improv scene as a ping pong table. In ping pong, you are required to hit the table on each volley. If you don't, you lose a point. You also generally want to hit the ball as fast as you can, so that it's difficult for your opponent to return, but you can't hit it so hard that it doesn't come down and bounce off the table.

In a scene, you want interesting, fun, even crazy things to happen. You want to "say yes" to the thing that might not happen on a regular day, but you still have to hit the table on every move.

"Not hitting the table" means not playing it real, which means you're doing something that feels false and weird and forced.

Here's an example from the improv group JV, showing how you can keep the scene real but still say yes to the unusual thing.

The monologist told a story of how he and his high school girlfriend had agreed to have sex, but he had to wait because he had agreed to go on a "stupid road trip with my stupid friends."

Off that story, Cissy Fenwick started this scene. She set up like she was driving a car, and began:

> **Cissy:** I just want to say, I know you're not having sex, but we're not stupid.

Team members Paul Welsh, Rene Gube, Casey Feigh, and Mary Holland joined in as passengers. Paul took the role of the person Cissy had just been talking to.

> **Paul:** What?

Rene: Yeah, Chris, you said we were your stupid friends.

Mary: You said you'd rather be having sex than spending time with us.

Paul: I meant it in the way that everyone means "stupid," like lightly resentful. It was no judgment on your intelligence!

Casey: C'mon, you think we're all stupid.

Paul: I wasn't calling you stupid. I was just saying, like, I was being a resentful teen. I wasn't being analytical about how smart you are!

Paul has kept the scene authentic by giving a reasonable response, and now that he's done that, he can go on to say yes to the endowment.

Paul: But if we're being honest, some...

Cissy: Some what, Chris?

Mary: Yeah, Chris, some what?

Paul: Someone in this car... is not smart.

Everyone in the car is shocked and offended. This is another way of "hitting the table"—framing that this statement is unusual.

Paul: If we're just being honest! If we're all being honest, and now that's what this trip is about.

Mary: *(voice becoming slightly dumb)* Yeah right. I'm smart! I know I'm smart, it's not me!

Cissy: *(also sounding confused)* Yeah, I know I'm smart!

Rene: *(carefully)* WHOM is it?

Casey: *(slowly, deliberately)* Perhaps we should go around... clockwise... starting with me... who is the... 12 spot?

Mary: Yeah, there's... five of us... in this car?

Casey: Madam I'm Adam! That's backwards and forwards the same! We call those... um...

And the rest of the scene became a contest of five dumb friends trying to prove they were not dumb. They started truthfully, introduced an unusual thing carefully, and then, once it was set, ran with it.

SAYING NO: PUMPING THE BRAKES

Another key factor to keeping your scenes real is learning how to say "no."

In improv, the main mantra is "yes and." You're supposed to say yes to everything weird. Right?

No.

Your character will very often not want to do something, and in those cases it is okay to say no. New improvisers and even experienced improvisers feel guilty saying no. You shouldn't. You just have to know how to do it correctly.

Let's think of improv as bicycling. "Saying yes" and moving the action forward is pedaling, and saying "no" is pumping the breaks. If all you do is use the brakes, then you're not going to go anywhere. You also can't really start off by hitting the brakes. Over the course of your ride, though, you'll absolutely need to hit the brakes at some point.

Say someone tells your character to do something crazy—you're a guy on a bus, and a stranger suggests that you rob a bank. You say "no."

But you do it as if you're hitting the brakes on a bike. You don't want to hit the brakes so hard that you stop the ride, so you just pump them a bit. You say "no" but you stay engaged in the conversation and stay suggestible. Maybe this person is going to be able to convince you to rob the bank. Stay open to that possibility. If the scene needs you to say yes, the offer will come around again soon. If you feel the scene grinding to a halt, find a way to pedal (make the unusual thing happen, and say yes).

You just have to make sure that it's your character who is saying no, and not you the actor. It can't be that you the actor are scared of doing something, like being committed to the scene. You have to be in the flow of the scene and committed, and once you are in that state, then there will just be times your character wants to say no. Don't feel bad for hitting the brakes.

And, again, I'm not talking about physically intrusive stuff like someone yelling too loud in your face. See "You Don't Have To Be Picked Up" in the "Be Brave" section.

When you're first learning to ride a bike, you hit the brakes more often because you're nervous about going fast, but as you get more comfortable, you'll find you need those brakes less.

YOU ALREADY KNOW THE REAL "WHY"

In improv you're often doing something before you really know why you're doing it. This is if you're doing it right. You react, and now you've done something.

That's great. The next step is realizing why you're doing something—the real, natural why that's inside of you, not the one you think you should have.

I saw a two-person class scene where one person said, "I want to run with the bulls in Spain."

The other person had this instinctive reaction and responded with just a tiny bit of disgust: "Ugh, not that."

I stopped the scene and said, "I love that. Why don't you want to run with the bulls?"

And the student felt guilty that he had "said no," and corrected himself: "I mean, I love running with the bulls."

I said, "No, I didn't want you to change your mind. It's okay you didn't like it. I just wanted to know why your character didn't like it."

Then the student thought about it too much. He tried to create a big, improbable backstory to explain his actions: "Maybe my father was killed by bulls?"

"No," I said. "That's not the reason. You had a reason—there's something you didn't like about the idea on a gut level. I'm just asking what that reason was. The one you already had."

And then he remembered what it felt like the moment he answered, and he said, "Because running with the bulls is something that jerks do?"

That was it. That was the real reason. That's the type of reason an audience can sense and will laugh at, when they see you realize and articulate it.

You say, "Ugh, not that," and then follow up with, "Don't be such a frat guy. Don't try to be so tough." It's your real, grounded answer.

When you have an instinctual, visceral reaction to something—it's probably the honest and true one. You just have to be able to say what that honest reaction is. Being able to stop, hold, and articulate your natural feelings is a hugely necessary skill in improv. It's very hard to do, and there are many people out there who can't do it.

Imagine your co-worker says they hate French Vanilla coffee, and you ask why. They'd look at you and say, "What do you mean *why?* I just do."

That's not enough in improv. You must be an honest reporter of your natural, unaffected feelings. Tricky. But it's way more important than doing a great accent, or being able to think of 20 movies from the 1940s, or even being able to emote a huge range of feelings.

Don't think about it, don't fix it—just say what you feel: the real "why."

MEMENTO AND SPLIT-BRAIN EXPERIMENTS

Here are two situations that explain what it should feel like in an improv scene when you are asked "why":

a. **In the movie *Memento*,** the main character cannot form new memories and thus is constantly in situations that are a surprise to him. Also, the scenes are shown in reverse chronological order, so the audience also does not know what caused them.

   At one point, he's being chased through a parking lot by someone shooting at him, and you hear him thinking, "Okay, so what's going on here?" He has to guess what's going on with context clues. He generally assumes that whatever is going on is because of something he's done, and that he meant for it to happen.

   That's how the improviser should approach scenes where they've been accused of something. They must assume that it's true, that they did something to create this situation, and then sense why they would have done such a thing.

b. **Split-Brain Experiments.** In the first half of the 20th century, when people suffered from epileptic seizures that were so intense they could not function, doctors might perform surgery to separate the hemispheres of their brains. The surgery would stop the seizures but leave the patient with a "split brain," meaning the two halves of the brain could not communicate directly.

   Doctors could then perform cool experiments like this: they'd cover the patient's ear on one side of his head, and tell him something that then only one side of his brain could receive. In one experiment, they made the patient cover his right ear, such that only the left ear was receiving information—and thus sending it only to the right brain (because the body and brain are crosswired that way). Then they said, "Okay, get up, switch to cover your other ear, and go to the next room." The man got up, switched to cover his left ear—so now the left brain was the only side that could "hear"—and started to walk to the next room.

   In the middle of this trip, the doctors stopped him and said, "Where are you going?" And the man said immediately, "To the bathroom."

The side of his brain that led him to speak (the left side) didn't really know where he was going, because it was the right side of his brain that had received that information. But in the heat of the moment he made his best guess as to where he was headed, and proclaimed it out loud.

That's what it's like to do improv. You're doing something, or you're being told that you're doing something, and you don't really know, at first, why. But you have to explain it. If you're a good actor, and you're in the moment, you will come up with a specific, true, and interesting reason. It will be related on some level to why *you* would have done such a thing.

TAKE THE LOCAL

Another important part of making your improv authentic is avoiding getting too crazy too fast.

This is a quote from UCB performer and teacher Neil Casey: "You can take the train to crazytown, but you have to take the local."

"Crazytown" is a term for when your scene has become so insane that it no longer makes sense, and it's not satisfying. Generally, "crazytown" is bad.

On the flip side, if you avoid any sort of unusual thing at all, your scenes will be boring.

Neil's quote points out that if you just heighten slowly, you can still have "crazy" things in your scene.

A common obstacle to keeping a scene authentic occurs when someone takes the funny thing and starts to heighten it too quickly.

For example, someone starts a scene by saying that they don't eat cereal because it's bad for you. Someone responds by saying, "Yeah, carbs are ruining our lives," and then someone else says, "Yeah, I haven't eaten cereal in 25 years!" Then someone tags everyone out and addresses a crowd, saying, "Let's burn down the grocery store!"

What started as a realistic moment then became a philosophy, and then became a silly scene with no grounding and no investment. It was heightened into senselessness.

The lesson is to go more slowly. If someone says they don't eat cereal because it's bad for you, just respond honestly what your character thinks. Maybe you can yes-and by saying, "Yeah, I've noticed that you're eating a lot better lately," and see where it goes. There's plenty of time to get to "crazytown" via local stops.

Here's a scene from the group Bangarang! They were doing scenes inspired by a monologist, who had made an offhand comment that "My cat would be a better driver than I am." Adam McCabe started a scene with Ryan Stanger as a guy who lets his cat drive.

For some groups, having a cat drive a car might be too silly or unrealistic, but Bangarang! manages the unusual thing carefully. Ryan protects the truthfulness of the scene by being completely stunned to see the cat drive.

> **Adam:** Oh, Danny boy, the pipes the pipes are calling! We drank too much, dude!

> **Ryan:** We did, we did!

> **Adam:** I can't drive, but don't sweat it. Let me get into my car, have my cat drive. My cat will drive us, dude! Get in!

Lauren Lapkus sits in the driver's seat as the cat. She uses excellent physical comedy to be at once blasé and an expert driver. Ryan is stunned and confused.

> **Ryan:** Nah, dude! That's too, I don't know, dude...

> **Adam:** My cat will drive us, dude! We can't drive, we're too drunk! Come on, dude!

> **Ryan:** Okay. You won't get arrested?

> **Adam:** My cat is awesome, dude, she drives everywhere.

Ryan shrugs his shoulders and gets in. He's been the voice of reason, but he doesn't want to stop the scene. Lauren starts driving. Ryan remains stunned.

> **Ryan:** What the fuck! Dude, I'm so drunk right now!

> **Adam:** Wanna go to Taco Bell? Let's go to Taco Bell!

From the backline teammate Betsy Sodaro does the voice of a Taco Bell cashier, coming out of a drive-thru intercom.

> **Betsy:** *(on mic)* Welcome to Taco Bell.

> **Adam:** I'll get two quesalupas, sub beans in for beef. *(to Ryan)* What do you want, dude?

> **Lauren:** *(meowing the order to the intercom)* Meow, meow, meow!

Like Ryan's, Betsy's initial reaction is to be truthful.

> **Betsy:** Wait, all I'm hearing is ping-ping-ping! What is it that you want?

Lauren "meows" more carefully, as Adam specifies his order.

> **Adam:** No lettuce. ("Meow.") Make sure she doesn't put lettuce on it. ("Meow.") What do you want, dude?

Jacob Reed on the backline sees a chance for a pattern and starts making meowing sounds coming from the intercom.

> **Speaker:** Meow! Meow! Meow!

And then Betsy explains this new unusual thing using the same logic that accompanied the first time we saw a cat doing a human's job.

Betsy: I'm sorry, I'm super drunk so I let my cat do my job. He's really good. Come on, keep doing it, Cookie! *(meows continue)* Meoooow! Meoooow!

Adam: We got our food! Thanks, dudes!

Lauren: Meow!

Adam: All right, pull out!

They leave.

Ryan: What the fuck!

At this point, Bangarang! has created a world where cats can do human things. Great physical comedy, patient pacing, and consistent justification have held the scene together.

Adam: What's wrong? You don't like that? You don't like the quesalupa?

Ryan: No, I'm scared of the cats, dude!

Ryan Meharry on the backline makes a police siren and approaches the car as a policeman. Toni Charline joins him as his partner.

Ryan: God! We're screwed!

Lauren, still as a cat, gestures for everyone in the car to be cool.

> **Adam:** Shut up, dude! Be cool!

> **Meharry:** I pulled you guys over to give you a random "Great Driving" commendation, but I see you have a cat driving this car.

> **Adam:** She's got a license!

> **Meharry:** May I see it?

Lauren gives the cop a license.

> **Ryan:** What the fuck!

Meharry looks over the license, then addresses his partner.

> **Meharry:** All right, I'm gonna run this. Felix, what do you think?

> **Toni:** Meow?

Usually you'd want to explain why a cat can drive and how it got a license. Or how a cat can be a policeman's partner. But Bangarang! got to crazytown in a controlled, patient way, explaining each step with either a truthful reaction or a fun justification.

SANFORD MEISNER ON ACTING

The legendary acting teacher Sanford Meisner has a book called *On Acting*. Most of the book is a description of an actual class he taught. You see the exercises he gives and the notes he offers, and you read his opinions of students' progress along the way. There are many passages that make for great advice for the improviser who wants to act more simply and powerfully.

In the first chapter, he asks his class to count the ceiling tiles in the room—to really do it. They all look up and start to count. Midway through, Meisner stops them. *Do you know what you look like?* he asks them. *You look like people counting ceiling tiles. Think how much worse it might have looked if you'd been asked to "act like" you were counting tiles.*

Make sure you're not filtering your behavior through some inadvertent "acting" modification. See if you can really be in the job interview, be in the conversation with your boyfriend, be pulled over by a cop.

Later in the book, Meisner asks his class to imagine a script that requires someone to say "ouch." What's the best way to get your scene partner to say "ouch?" And then he pinches one of his students. "Ouch," he says.

It's not about physically hurting someone; it's about really provoking someone. You want a reaction? You can provoke it.

We know how to be powerfully affecting presences who get reactions out of people. We do it every day with the people in our lives. Bring it to the stage.

BE YOURSELF

A powerful way to make scenes feel truthful and real is to simply be yourself.

Some night in the fall of 2000, my classmates and I were sitting in the Irish pub and UCB Theatre hangout McManus, trying to figure out what made The Swarm so good.

The Swarm was the undisputed best team at the UCB at the time. Every show they did seemed effortless, artful, and hilarious. They had the most original takes on every idea and executed them in surprising ways. How did they do it? What did they have?

At some point, we were joined by Rob Riggle, an amazing improviser who was then a member of Respecto Montalban, the other great team of this era. Part of the fun of going to McManus after shows was the chance to hang out with senior performers and shamelessly make them talk about improv with you. We asked Rob why he thought The Swarm was so good. He said, "I think whenever one of them enters a scene, they bring their whole self with them."

In the years since that night I've noticed the same thing about almost every great improviser. Their real selves—their temperaments, their opinions, their reactions—are a huge part of every character they play. By the end of the set, you feel like you know them.

I've heard teachers use the phrase "is someone home?" to test if a character is specific. Is there more to that character than just the expected, iconic things? If the teacher is just talking about grading papers and wanting new textbooks, there might not be anyone home. If the teacher tries to explain U.S. history in terms of characters from a reality show that he loves, then it feels like there's someone home.

As an actor, you'll never have more experience playing any character besides yourself, so you should use it in your improv. It's what makes your scenes unique and surprising but still truthful.

WHAT WOULD YOU SAY?

A very common note from improv teachers is, "What would *you* say here?" They're asking you to give the commonsense reaction to whatever is going on in the scene. They want you to notice what the audience is noticing and speak to it. They also want to know if you are observing something that most people wouldn't observe—something particular to your sensibilities.

But it's not as simple as it sounds. What they are really asking you to do is something a bit trickier. You also have to say yes to all the facts, be brave about any acting choices being asked of you, and adhere to the principles of KNOW, CARE, and SAY.

So what you're actually being asked is: "After having said yes to all the facts, and doing any brave acting tasks at hand, and also presuming that you will choose to KNOW what's going on, CARE about it, and are willing to SAY what you think—now, what would *you* say?"

In the "Reps" section of "Be Present," I said the hardest acting job is often just acting "like a normal person." It's also surprisingly hard to "act like yourself," but that's what you must do to make your improv scenes compelling. What is it, given that this situation is happening, that you would say? To do that, you have to be able to relate to the scene, no matter what.

Here's a scene between improvisers Rhona Cleary and Ruha Taslimi, where Rhona has cooked and served her own cat as a meal.

Rhona: I see you enjoyed dinner. That was my cat you just ate.

Ruha: *(throws up)*

Rhona: Aw, come on. You're exaggerating. It's not that bad. People have eaten cats in history. They wouldn't be alive if they didn't!

Ruha: You just rescued that cat! You cooked that cat?

Rhona: Wait a minute, I'm not the villain here. That cat had feline AIDS. It wasn't going to have a great life.

Ruha: Even if somehow you do believe you were sparing that cat, why would you feed me a cat without telling me?

Rhona: You are the most adventurous person I know! I've seen you eating tripe! I've seen you eat haggis!

Ruha: I knew I was eating those things! You thought, "Ooh, I know what Stacy would love! She's gonna be so surprised that she ate a cute cat!"

Rhona: Look, get over the cute part. It was unhealthy, it was dying.

Ruha: They can treat feline AIDS! There's lots of cats that live with it!

Rhona: They have miserable lives! Look, I believe in medically assisted suicide. It was the same thing. I'm surprised at your response! I thought this would be one of those things that we'd both look back on and laugh about!

Ruha plays it truthfully, though she does not leave and continues to engage Rhona. Rhona plays it "as if" she had merely given her friend an exotic new food. They're not inventing elaborate reasons to "solve" the unusual thing, but instead are relating to the scene using the way they behave in real life.

They are both grounded. Ruha grounded to her real self. Rhona to the way people behave when introducing a new exotic food.

This is where empathy comes into play. Your job is to take all these feelings and fold them into a nice simple reaction. Maybe in real life you have a sales job and are intimidated by dealing with customers, and that dread is dominating what you feel. Maybe you're also so excited about doing this particular show that your mechanic is also excited. Maybe the other actor on stage with you is a friend with whom you frequently do "pretend hostile" bits, so you could act the same way right now. And what if the suggestion was something very leading, like "peace treaty"? You'll have feelings about that, too.

When we say "make a choice" at this moment, you're not so much making a choice from all possible choices that a human being could make, or that a writer could make. You're picking a true feeling from this soup inside of you and letting it grow. You respond with a dash of real (pick one) trepidation, excitement, remorsefulness, irritation, attraction, friendliness. The audience can feel that it comes from a real place, from you.

When we zoom in on this moment it may seem hard, but this actually becomes very easy. Improv lets you be yourself in every situation that you could imagine. With practice, you become very fast at bringing your real self into any scene. When improv scenes turn into honest conversations where your real feelings are in play, the audience knows it, and the scenes become specific and fascinating.

THE SECOND BIG CHOICE

The second big choice of a scene is often the first one where you make your own personal mark.

The first big choice you make is frequently simple. You get a suggestion, and that gives you a direction. Say the suggestion is "holidays." Someone initiates by rolling what seems to be a big ball of snow. That's the first big choice.

Then the two actors spend the next few lines clarifying what that means.

> Help me lift this onto the rest of the snowman.

Okay, it's a snowman.

> Sure, here you go. Looks good.

> Think Mom's done with dinner yet?

Okay, they're siblings, in their front yard.

Those choices all come in a bunch, pretty easily, and they're really just part of that first big choice, which came right off the suggestion. Even though you're a few lines in, and we've learned a bunch, you've really only made one choice and then very nicely clarified it.

What you need now is to make your second big choice. This one is deceptively hard.

You don't get another suggestion, so there is no "right" answer. This next choice is the first one that you are really making all on your own, and it will feel like something new, so people are often shy to make it.

At this point in our example, people will just end up saying the word "snowman" a million times, until the teacher stops the scene and says, "It's not about the snowman."

This is where long-form improv becomes art, rather than just a game of wits. You're not just fulfilling a clearly outlined set of rules: you are making a choice, and it will come from you. The audience gets to hear the things you think about making snowman, or siblings being together, or families—something personal and specific to you.

Ian Roberts uses a technique called "flashing." He points out that almost any move from one actor will trigger in the other actor some kind of memory or association. It will flash right away with very little thought. If you pay attention, you can "catch" that flash and use it in your scene. This will give you your second choice, and it will be using your unique experiences to do so.

In the "making a snowman" scene, you need something like:

- you're proud of having made a snowman because it's such a "normal kid" thing to do, as opposed to socially awkward, or
- your mom kicked you out of the house to play outside because she wanted to have sex with your father, or
- this is the first time you and your brother have done something without fist-fighting, or
- your grandfather would have been proud of you because he loved snowmen so much.

These all feel a bit out of nowhere. Nothing said in the first few lines implies any of those could be coming, but they're coming from memories and associations from your life, or things you've read or talked about.

I saw a scene that started with the suggestion "beauty." The first actor, Colin McGurk, comes out and mimes that he is sculpting something. Another actor, Gwen Mesco, joins him.

Colin: Nice, right?

Gwen: I love you, I support you, but... that's dirt.

That is not a denial; it's a difference of opinion. And Player A yes-ands it.

Colin: No! It's *gonna* be something! It's gonna be life. You know? That's a garden. And I *did* that.

Gwen: That's great, Gary.

Here's where they need a bit more. Something else that's both related to the situation, but also born of the player's own interests.

Colin: We're gonna be so healthy! I put in compost.

> **Gwen:** You put in compost?

> **Colin:** Yeah!

> **Gwen:** So we're gonna grow lettuce and it's going to be made out of human feces and pizza roll leftovers?

> **Colin:** You can compost anything, baby! Everything's compost!

And then a player from the backline, Kristina Nikolic, walked on and dumped a wheelbarrow full of trash.

> **Kristina:** Neighbor, how's it going? Just taking out the trash.

> **Colin:** Thanks, brother! *(then to Gwen)* I asked Larry to dump his trash in our garden.

> **Gwen:** Those are 17 beer cans!

> **Colin:** Yeah, Larry has a drinking problem.

The ability to make that second choice (and third and fourth and however many you need) is essential. It sounds simple, and often is, but many improvisers get stuck when they've unpacked everything they get out of the suggestion.

BE AUTHENTIC EXERCISES

TRUTHFUL AT ALL COSTS

Try doing a series of scenes like this. Two people up. Whoever initiates must make a big choice. Something unusual, fantastical, or strange. The responder simply has to act exactly as they would in real life.

Beware of people acting unrealistic just to "say yes." Here's a scene between improvisers Brock Bivens and Michael Hanggi.

> **Brock:** I gotta tell you something. Last night I was abducted by aliens. It was a classic silver thing like you see in the movies. It pulled me right up into the spaceship from my bed. Performed weird acts on me.

> **Michael:** *(deeply concerned)* Oh man, are you... are you okay?

I stopped the scene. That's not what you would say if a friend told you they were kidnapped by aliens. That's what's said by an improviser who is under pressure to "say yes." But I'm asking for a truthful response.

> **Brock:** They took me up there, they laid me on a bed. They performed, like, surgeries on me, they cut me open. And now I'm here! I just woke up, I was in my bed.

> **Michael:** Wait a minute. Sit down. *(Player A sits.)* Dude, I'm, like, worried about you, man.

Brock: I'M kinda worried about me! It's like I'm the only one who saw it, so I, like, I feel insane! I saw them! They were grey! They had the big eyes. And they were small! Like this big, and they walked around me, and they poked and they looked, and you're just like, "What's going on?" And I was, like, is this how my life ends? IS this life?

Michael: Dude, um, maybe we should go, like, talk to a specialist. Someone who can help you with this?

In this exercise, you can dismiss opinions that people try to pin on you, you can ask questions, you can refuse to believe things, and you can choose not to care! You also do not have to find the initiation unusual if you don't, like this beginning between Zach Pyke and Sommer Branham.

Zach: Mom, I've decided I'm never going to school again!

Sommer: Oh, honey. You'll learn to like school.

Sommer didn't find it weird for her child to say that, and she reacted naturally. Great! No problem.

A few caveats you'll have to point out: the responder cannot leave and must engage the person, and you cannot change any facts. If the weird thing is evident, you should believe it, but have a truthful reaction. Here's one between actors Robert Woo and Brad Cameron.

Robert: *(shoots gun at player)* Did that bullet just bounce off of you, man?

Brad: Don't tell anybody!

Robert: What? Stay away from me!

Brad: Don't tell anybody! I come from the planet Nangongongon! I come in peace—don't tell anyone!

Remember: "Saying yes" to the weird thing is pedaling, and expressing skepticism and "saying no" is like hitting the brakes. True, we need to be pedaling more than braking, but you do need to brake sometimes. Here's a scene from actors Sommer Branham and Jake Minton.

Sommer: So, babe, for dinner tonight, I kinda wanted to change things up. I got a peacock. And will you cut it up for me? I'll take care of the salad.

Jake: Babe, where did you get this?

Sommer: The neighbor's backyard. They have a couple of them. They look like pests. So I thought I was helping them.

Jake: Babe, we have to put this back.

Sommer: It's already dead. We're not putting it back.

Jake: I can see that it's dead. We can just sort of... I mean... I mean it sounds good.

Sommer: Doesn't it? Healthy protein.

Jake: Yeah. I'm just a little nervous. I mean… you have a peacock recipe? We have chicken in the freezer!

Sommer: I wanted to change things up! And he walked in front of my car. Wait, I'm pretty sure this is a boy, right, because of the long feathers?

Jake: I don't know! Wait, you ran this thing down with your car?

You can see in this scene the husband has room to be won over if that's what the scene needs. But he's being real. The wife has a reason for her behavior that's plausible without being so reasonable it kills the fun.

The actor playing the husband has a good sense of what his character knows: he doesn't know if it's a male peacock, but he notices and is alarmed when his wife said she hit it with her car.

The actors are reliable reporters of what's going on. They are engaged with the scene and using their own sensibilities. It's fun! Oh man, is it ever so good when they are allowed to play truthfully.

OBJECT INTO POINT OF VIEW

A strong point of view underlies an authentic scene. An improviser should be able to fish a good point of view out of any situation, no matter how mundane. This exercise practices that.

Everyone up in a circle. Someone starts by miming an object, saying what it is, and giving it to someone else in the circle.

"Stapler," they say, and give it to someone.

Whoever receives it does the following to create a POV from the object:

- This is OBJECT.
- It stands for IDEA.
- IDEA is important to me because (say 3–4 sentences as a character who really values IDEA).
- Then they cap it by holding up their mimed object and saying IDEA.

They might say this:

- This is a STAPLER.
- It stands for HOLDING THINGS TOGETHER.
- HOLDING THINGS TOGETHER is important to me because, well, I guess I think there's nothing as important as family. Keep your money, your power, your everything. All I care about is family.
- HOLDING THINGS TOGETHER.

For the 3–4 sentences, it should be done in character, and the reasons why the thing is important should refer to the character's philosophy, not external circumstances. Avoid reasons like, "I believe in holding things together because I was once trapped in a flood."

Practice the useful tool of taking a mundane detail and inferring a point of view from it.

START GENERAL, GET SPECIFIC

Another way to relate to a scene is to start with the most general version of the character, and then mix in more and more of your real self as you go. This makes the character more specific and also makes it easier to perform.

For example, someone starts a scene by accusing you of being a bad husband who stays at work too late. Start by saying the things we expect someone in that position to say. "C'mon, honey, you're being too sensitive," or "I'm just overwhelmed at work right now. We have a big project."

Then make it personal to you. Why are *you* late for things? What is it about *you* that makes you stay at something too long when you know there's someone waiting for you? "I overschedule myself. I just want to please everybody." Or: "I guess I just think it's not that big a deal to be half an hour late. It's just... not that big a deal." Or: "I feel good at work. I feel comfortable there. I'm the big king shit there, and I like it there." Take it from your real life.

It doesn't matter if you've never been married, or even if you've never had a day job. The general situation is one you've been in, so you can relate to it and mix in your real self.

HOW DID YOU BECOME A [BLANK]?

This is an exercise in taking a situation that seems impossible and making it seem plausible.

Two people up. One says to the other, "So, how did you get to be a [blank]?" where [blank] is any job: auto mechanic, deep sea diver, veterinarian, anything—but preferably something far away from what the person being asked really is.

The person then explains how they got that job, but the trick is to use as much of their real life as they can. Use real details from your life until you have to start branching off into an alternate life where you got this supposed job.

Let's say it's, "So how did you get to be a mailman?" You can't just say, "I graduated from college, and then I realized I loved the mail and so I became a mailman!" No, that's not how people get jobs, generally.

Take a moment and think about what could have really happened to make you a mailman.

Mine would be this: "I graduated from college as a journalism major *(true)*, but when I graduated the economy was terrible and there were no good jobs in almost any field *(true)*. My friends and I were sitting around and someone pointed out that a job in civil service would be nice because it's so structured *(not true, but could have happened)*. Pay raises are small, but kind of guaranteed if you do anything close to a decent job. And there's good benefits. So, even though it seemed 'beneath' a college graduate, I applied for a job and I got it *(not true, but doesn't sound insane)*. Then I started getting promotions. I'm really organized *(true)* and I kinda like losing myself in fixed tasks *(true)*."

Then end it with the person who just described how they became a [blank] giving a surprising where for the scene. After explaining how you became a mailman, say, "Anyway, I'm here to get my car washed." That's just for fun and does not contribute to anything.

BE FUNNY

You're never supposed to say "be funny" when teaching improv. It puts a lot of pressure on people. It makes them act too crazy. And it seems to insult the art of being truthful and committed on stage.

But here's the bad news: to be good at improv, you *have* to be funny. It's not as fundamental a skill as listening and understanding and agreeing, but it is definitely an essential one. You have to have funny ideas, good timing, and a reliable radar of what is unusual.

You will be a good, helpful improviser if you simply commit and act truthfully. But you will not be a great one.

To be a great one, you must be funny.

One of my favorite moments at an improv workshop took place during one taught by UCB co-founder Matt Besser, in the summer of 2005.

It was in the UCB offices, which at that time were three rooms over the Malibu Diner on 23rd Street. The main office—where the artistic director and school supervisor and others sat—was in the middle, and there was a classroom on either side of it, one to the north and one to the south. The northern classroom stored all the costumes used for the UCB's sketch show, and had a cot where Besser would sometimes crash when he was in town from LA, as he was at this time. The southern room was smaller, a bit neater, and had what I remember as about 14 radiators that pumped full blast year-round, including the middle of July. We were in that one.

It was during the Del Close Marathon, the annual festival/homecoming at UCB, where there are improv shows and workshops 24 hours a day for three days to honor Del, legendary improv director and teacher and patron saint of the UCB. This meant that the workshop had a mixture of UCB superfans, out-of-town newbies, and a few teachers, of which I was one. We were all exhausted from having been up all night, many of us hungover.

Besser walked in, presumably having just grabbed a few hours of sleep on his cot two rooms away. We all sat up a bit straighter, intimidated to face one of the UCB himself, a founder of our theater and a notoriously hard-to-impress teacher. He'd moved to LA, so few of us had had him for a class.

Besser sat in a chair at the front of the room and lounged way back. He had on an Arkansas Razorbacks basketball team t-shirt, baggy jeans, and beat-up sneakers, loosely tied. He looked tired and his expression seemed skeptical by default. Though he was technically facing the class, he seemed to be gazing at a spot on the floor just a few feet in front of him. It wasn't clear class had started until he started talking.

"So why do you guys want to do improv?"

Silence. Then someone timidly raised their hand. "I want to learn how to be in the moment."

Besser nodded. "Be in the moment, okay. Anyone else?"

Answers started coming a bit more confidently. "To learn how to play it real." "To support my scene partner." "To have a group mind." "To find truth in comedy."

Besser nodded at all of them. After the answers stopped coming, he raised his eyebrows and said, "No one here wants to be funny?"

We paused and stared back, then at each other, then back again. Besser seemed irritated. Were we in trouble?

"Nobody likes... comedy? Nobody was a fan of comedy and then saw an improv show and thought it was funny and said 'I want to be funny'?'"

We slowly nodded. Yes, we wanted to be funny. We liked funny things.

"I bet you all, before you wanted any of those things you just said, just wanted to be funny. It's good. You should want to be funny. Improv is funny. Right? Okay, two people up."

And we proceeded to have a Matt Besser workshop, which is an exciting, educational, inspirational, and intimidating experience. It was one of my favorites ever.

It was the first time an improv teacher ever told me directly that it was okay to want to be funny.

I understand how the culture came to abhor the words "joke" and "funny." That's because improv is first and foremost an actor's medium. It requires listening, agreement, and commitment before all else. Given that many people who get into improv have very little acting background, you must emphasize these things—listening, agreement, commitment—many, many times before your students can really start to do it.

The students who try to make jokes and who seem to want badly to be funny—well, at first they can only do those things by breaking reality, by selling out their scene partner, by making jokes that insult the integrity of the scene itself.

The tendency is to coach away from that and say, "Don't worry about being funny; just support. Be truthful and say what you would really say, not some joke."

But teachers can go too far in this regard. We forget the ultimate goal: to come back from your time practicing good acting and make a comedy show.

You can get there however you want. Fast or slow. In one scene or in 45 of them. Use tag-outs, or keep it a monoscene. Have an opening or don't. Two people or 20. There's lots of ways, all valid.

But if you're putting a show up in a comedy theater, the audience should laugh or you didn't do it right. That's not heresy, that's respect. Respect for the audience that came to see a show. Respect for how hard it is to make something that's funny. Respect for the tradition of theater and writing and comedy in LA and NY and Chicago and every other place where someone put up a sign that said "improv show tonight."

SURPRISE

Being funny is a state of mind, and the main ingredient for that state is a hunger to surprise: to give the answer we didn't think of; to react with an emotion we didn't expect; to care more than we predicted; to be more specific than necessary.

Though I'm talking about being funny in scenes right now, if you're truly a funny person you should want to be surprising all the time in your life. You want to walk up to a vending machine at work, then realize that your co-worker is watching you, and instead of buying anything, at the last second give the machine a high-five and walk away. A friend asks if you want to try a bite of his meal, and you take the entire steak off his plate and put it on yours.

You should want to do things like this all the time.

Note that I say you should *want* to. It doesn't mean you should always do it in a scene. Surprise too much and you will just be denying offers. You will be uncooperative. You will be unsupportive. We don't need a funny move on every line. That would probably be too unreal, and almost definitely annoying.

Still, though, you should feel, at all times, a tickling desire to zag when everyone thinks you're going to zig. Most times you will not give in to that desire, but it should be there.

You want to be funny? Then you want surprise.

I saw a scene in which John Gemberling was a superintendent scolding a teacher played by Brett Gelman.

Gelman said, "Don't tell me what to do, Superintendent Shithead!"

Gemberling responded, "You're pronouncing my name wrong, it's...."

I want to pause here and say that this is actually a very common response to being given a silly name. Someone calls you "Dr. Hardass" and you say, "It's actually Har-daz-say." I see it all the time.

But to my surprise, Gemberling finished with, "...it's pronounced Superin-*TYNE*-dent Shithead."

Oh man, did I laugh. Correcting the pronunciation of "superintendent" I did not expect. He used a hack comedy move, but in an unhacky way. I loved it. I thought the scene was going to be so predictable, and then that line showed me I was in the hands of genuinely funny people.

And more importantly: *he said yes to the offer.* He did not deny anything. This guy said his name was "Shithead," and he did not change that at all.

That's the real trick: being surprising *while still saying yes.* Your two desires are at war. The mischievous comedian wants to be surprising—to say no, almost—but the dutiful improviser wants to say yes and to support.

This is where wit comes in. Can you satisfy your constant desire to surprise while also fulfilling your obligation as a good improviser to make things true? Can you say yes in a way we did not expect?

A common resolution of this struggle is to say yes, but with a twist. Someone will say, "You haven't been working here that long!" And the person will respond, "What, it's been two whole weeks!"

Another way to be surprising while still saying yes is the technique called "A-to-C." That's a term for making a bit of a big jump from the last idea. It's generally applied to getting surprising ideas from a suggestion.

I saw a scene where the suggestion was "vegetarian." To start, Chris Gethard stepped off the back line and mimed heaving a bucket of paint on someone, while saying, "Fur is murder!"

That right there is pretty funny. It's surprising in a satisfying way. Instead of an obvious start off of vegetarian, like just sitting down to dinner, he made the A-to-C leap to make a scene about someone protesting for animal rights. It fits, but it's a surprise.

The response to this initiation from Zach Woods was even better: "C'mon! This is a gorilla suit!"

That player said yes to the fact that he is wearing fur, but he made it surprising: he's wearing the silliest, most harmless kind of fur you could think of.

I saw another scene between Stephan Bekiranov and Jon Daly, where Stephan was a father talking to his son.

Stephan: Son, I understand you want to change your name. You're not happy with being Jon?

Jon: No, Dad. And I already have changed it. It's 'Dave.' *(off Stephan's look of surprise)* You thought it was going to be something crazy!

Now, you can already tell we're infringing on the realm of denying each other. The father wanted the son to have a crazy name, and the son, in order to be more surprising, chose a "normal" name. Then the player commented on the scene from within it.

Yes, we are walking a line here. If it's funny, though, isn't that okay? *Don't you want to be funny?*

A good guiding principle should be: don't ever change hard facts. If the dad said you changed your name, you did. If you are endowed as "Superintendent Shithead," then that's your name. You can still usually find a way to change some other specific or some opinion to stay surprising.

Another guiding principle is: don't twist too much at the start. We need some nice clean yeses in order to connect. Remember the advice about catching the inbound pass. We generally need to connect first before we unleash our desire to make surprising moves.

(The example above about the gorilla suit came in the second line, but that was a veteran team, with players who were good enough to take care of their yeses and their connections after that move.)

You should have this mischievous urge to surprise at all times. But many times you will keep that urge in check in order to support the scene, to let the obvious thing happen, and to let everyone get on the same page.

PATTERNS

The other thing a funny mind craves is patterns. Make the interesting and funny parts happen again.

In the movie *Talladega Nights* (co-written by longtime improviser Adam McKay), Will Ferrell plays a racecar driver who at one point is insisting to a few of his friends that his legs are paralyzed. To prove it, he plunges a pocket knife into his thigh. He immediately realizes that he is wrong—that his legs are not paralyzed—so he screams in pain. Thereafter follows a quick montage of his friends trying to get the knife out of his thigh. And one of the things they try is *putting a second pocket knife into the wound.*

Insane. Irrational. And so funny.

Patterns are musical. They touch the same parts of our brains that rhymes and rhythm do. Funny scenes have them. Funny people are drawn to them.

The danger is that they collide with our desire to be authentic. The first time something funny or interesting happens, it's probably nicely in the flow of things, but making it happen again requires breaking reality a bit. The audience won't mind, because patterns are satisfying to our tool-making brains.

Trained actors who are new to improv will have trouble. They're so practiced at making moments authentic that they forget to coax the weird parts to happen again, in almost exactly the same form.

Keep an ear out for unique phrasings, and if they are fun, repeat them.

Here are improvisers Dennis Curlett, Michael Gardner, and Danny Cymbal playing contestants on *Wheel of Fortune.* On the show, you have to guess a phrase a letter at a time. In this scene, they make a pattern out of figuring out one letter, then attempting to solve the puzzle with whatever nonsense phrase has been spelled using only the letters guessed to that point.

Dennis: I'd like to buy a vowel. An "A."

Michael: Are there any "A"s?

Danny: *(doing sound effects, a "ding" for each "A" found)* Ding! Ding! Ding! Ding! Ding! Ding!

Dennis: I'd like to solve the puzzle! "AAAAAAAAAAAAAAAAA!"

Danny: *(sound effect for a wrong guess)* Bzzt.

Michael: Oh, it appears that was incorrect.

Danny spins.

Michael: Okay, it's $200.

Danny: Uh, "Y."

Michael: Do we have any "Y"s?

Dennis: Ding!

Danny: I'd like to solve please.

Michael: Okay.

Danny: What is "YAAAAAAAAAAAAAAAAAA!"

Michael: Bzzt. Well, it appears that was incorrect. Back to you, John.

Dennis spins.

Michael: That's $800.

Dennis: "P."

Michael: Do we have any "P"s?

> **Danny:** *(very long beat, then)* Ding!

> **Dennis:** I want to solve the puzzle. Is it "YAAAAAAAAAAAAAAAAAAAP!"

A beat, no sound effects come from anyone.

> **Michael:** That's correct! You solved the puzzle!

Notice that they're not really worried about who wins. They are focused on continuing the pattern. Notice also that when they think the pattern is used up, they declare the puzzle solved so they can move on.

BE IRONIC

One of the clearest ways to have something funny in your improv scene is to have something ironic. It's not the only way, but it's among the most direct routes to funniness.

By ironic I mean someone or something behaving in the opposite way from how we expect. A drill sergeant screaming nice things. A Mother Superior tearing apart her hotel room in a rage. A teacher burning a book. A bully cheering on the math team.

Or the setting could be ironic. You could have a drill sergeant acting just like a drill sergeant, but he's in a yoga class.

Simply being mean or stupid in character is sometimes ironic—but not necessarily. A move is ironic only when it's contrary to expectations. It's not someone acting arbitrarily or randomly—it's someone acting the opposite of their expected way. So, it's not a drill sergeant who's really into dubstep, or is otherwise "weird." Rather, it's a drill sergeant being forgiving, or being against rules, or being soft-spoken. Gilbert and Sullivan called this "the topsy-turvy."

I bring this up because I see a lot of improvisers do scenes where weird things are happening, but the things aren't really funny—because they aren't actually ironic.

Example: Two improvisers establish that they're on a deserted island, and they're moaning about how much they want to get rescued.

Then a third improviser enters and says he's flyering for Subway sandwiches. Would they like a flyer?

It feels funny. The rest of the class laughs, and everyone in the scene feels their eyebrows raise: *hey, this is it! This is what our scene is going to be about!*

But then the couple asks, "Where did you come from?" The guy passing out the flyers says, "Just over the hill." The couple says, "There's a town over there?" The guy says, "Oh yeah, there's a whole town." Then a fourth improviser comes on and invites them to a dance at the local club in the town. I think a fifth one came on and said he was a doctor with food and plane tickets to the mainland.

This is common in scenes. Something unusual happens, so everyone makes more of it, but they lose what's funny.

Everything working out for the couple unusually well: not funny. A couple having been so dumb they didn't notice a city: not funny.

If you're attuned, however, to looking for irony, or something opposite, or topsy-turvy, the scene would go differently.

The first thing: the guy flyering. That's not just good luck for the couple— that's someone who is not where he belongs. Flyering on a deserted island: that's irony. That's funny. Now you need someone to come on raising money for Greenpeace, and a census taker, and then a guy who sells traffic lights.

Or maybe you don't need walk-ons: the guy with the flyers keeps trying to get the couple interested in Subway. He offers coupons and describes the nutritional value. He talks about how he needs to reach huge crowds of people. He offers discounts for groups of 10 or more. The couple look around the deserted island and see no one.

Other ways it could go and still be ironic:

- The guy flyers the couple, and they are relieved because the only thing they missed from civilization is being flyered.

- All those walk-ons I described in the original scene happen and the couple still believes they won't be rescued; they give up hope.

Ultimately, you don't think, "What would be ironic here?" while you're doing improv. That's too heady. What actually happens is that you feel something funny take place and you help make more of the funny thing. Look for whoever is acting differently than we expect.

BE A GOOD VOICE OF REASON

It's common to describe the "voice of reason" as the "straight man." I try not to use that term because I do not necessarily advise playing the voice of reason in a "straight" way, meaning flat or unaffected. I think the voice of reason should often be charged up, energetic, engaged, and fun.

In "Who's On First?" Lou Costello is the voice of reason. He has the rational point of view, which is that "Who" must be a pronoun and can't be the actual name of someone. Bud Abbott is playing the unusual side of things, and he's doing it in a "straight" way.

The "voice of reason" is the person in the scene who points out the absurdity. They represent the audience, asking the logical and reasonable questions about whatever is funny.

To tweak a premise described earlier, with Amy Poehler hunting Ian Roberts: If someone says to you, "Honey, we've talked about how our marriage is getting a little, well, stagnant. So, starting this evening, in order to spice things up, I am going to hunt you."

If you say, "I do not want to be hunted, sweetheart. That's dangerous!" you are taking the "voice of reason" role. You're pushing back against the funny idea in order to call attention to how weird it is. That's called "framing" the unusual thing, or "calling it out."

Now, if voices of reason get too forceful or dominant or fussy, they can ruin a scene. Here's how to be a good one.

Be Curious: The voice of reason should always want to know more. "Why do you want to hunt me?" If the other person is stuck for a reason, you should have enough empathy to suggest one. "Sweetheart, is this because the guys at work say you're not manly enough?"

Be Almost Convinced: The funniest posture for a voice of reason is to sit right on the brink of being convinced. No matter how insane the idea, you are almost ready to give it a shot. Better than a hard "no" is a careful "I don't *think* so...." I was on a two-person improv team with a friend who, like me, was often a straight man in scenes. We called ourselves "The Furrowed Brows," because that was such a common expression when dealing with an insane idea.

Point Out The Funniest Dumb Consequences: Writers and analytical people make great voices of reason because they quickly see the funniest consequences of a funny idea—the ones that are true but that we the audience have not yet considered. In response to the above "I'm going to hunt you," you could say, "You don't want to do that. You would be such a terrible widower." Or: "And you'll clean up my body? I doubt it." Or: "You couldn't defend yourself against a murder charge—you're a terrible liar."

If You're Ever "Winning," Back Off: Generally speaking, if the voice of reason wins, the scene feels smug and boring. We don't want you to "win" the scene. We just want you to explore and challenge the idea to get more fun out of it. Be ready to take your foot off the brakes and let the other person get their way in order for the scene to continue.

Try to strike one of these three basic tones as a voice of reason:

Be As Dry As Toast: Adopt a reasonable, moderate tone and engage the insanity with a disarming calmness.

Have Just A Small Stick Up Your Rear: Be perturbed, prissy, and put off by the crazy person.

Be Insanely Freaked Out: Be completely taken apart by the craziness! Scream! This is the nuttiest idea you have ever heard of! This will ruin everything!

Regardless of your tone, you will still be curious, you will still be almost convinced, and you will remain engaged and changeable.

Here's a scene between performers Heather Woodward and Lilan Bowden. There was a story in their opening about how in college someone burned their lips on a very tart pineapple. Someone responded with, "So your crazy night in college was eating a whole pineapple?" After the opening, Lilan started this scene:

Lilan: Freshman year!

Heather: Yeah! This dorm is great.

Lilan: There's so many cute guys on this campus. Oh my God. Hey, so Sigma Nu is having a party tonight. I was thinking of going. I don't know. It's crazy. I've never really been outside my hometown so this is like nuts. I was thinking about going there, and, like, I don't know, getting drunk...

Heather: Yeah, doing shots!

Lilan: Maybe having my first lesbian experience...

Heather: Oh my God, yeah.

Lilan: Or, there's also, like, a fruit stand, like, down in the quad, that's selling papayas and pineapples and stuff.

Heather: You're going to fill that pineapple with vodka, aren't you?

Lilan: No. I was thinking about purchasing one and then taking it back here and then cutting it up...

Heather: *(intrigued)* Okay, go on.

Lilan: ...and then consuming the whole thing!

Heather: You didn't mention any partying in that description.

Lilan: No. That would be my second option I think. Go to Sigma Nu, get blasted, see who and what I can touch.

Heather: Yeah! New experiences!

Lilan: Or... maybe just down that pineapple.

Heather: Why does pineapple meet the level of partying?

Lilan: Well, you know, I've never done a ton of stuff before. And I was in Econ today and thinking, "I've never eaten a whole pineapple," and you know, college is the time to try stuff!

Heather: Oh God, you grew up on that houseboat.

Lilan: Yeah, this is my first time on solid land.

Heather does a great job as the voice of reason. She frames what is unusual, asks pertinent questions, all the while staying curious, intrigued, and invested.

BE UNNECESSARILY SPECIFIC

I like improvisers who like words. They pepper their scenes with deliberately chosen phrases and surprising adjectives. They say things like, "I feel like a hummingbird!" or "What a zesty pâté!" They don't do scenes about "cancer;" they say "non-Hodgkin's lymphoma."

It surprises. It adds information. It's a choice. And it's pretty easy to do.

Especially in the 10 million scenes you will do where you have to order dinner, be fast enough to order a specific dish. Don't think of it beforehand; just look up and say the most specific meal you can: "Yes, I'll have grilled tilapia and chilled white wine."

Here's a scene between Hillary Matthews and Rose O'Shea, where the specifics make the scene. It starts with Rose as a housewife getting a divorce from her husband, Hank, and Hillary trying to reassure her.

Rose proposes becoming fans of the band Insane Clown Posse. As you may know, Insane Clown Posse is a real rap duo that holds an annual festival called "The Gathering of the Juggalos," featuring horror-themed, drug-tolerant parties and close-to-physically-violent wrestling matches.

In addition to the great specifics, notice how often Rose and Hillary literally say the word "yes" to confirm new information, and how often they make patterns by re-using the phrases they've enjoyed.

> **Rose:** I want to thank you for how supportive you've been through this divorce, Diane. I just… it's like I don't know who I am anymore after Hank.

> **Hillary:** These are growing pains! We don't expect it, but we take it one day at a time.

> **Rose:** I just want to get out of here. And I want to… oh, this is probably a terrible idea…

> **Hillary:** No! Let's get you out of here! We want that pep back in your step, girlfriend.

> **Rose:** Here's what I want. I want to get a bottle of rosé.

> **Hillary:** *(excited)* Okay, I'm listening!

> **Rose:** Get in the Subaru.

> **Hillary:** Yes.

Rose: Drive up the coast.

Hillary: Yes.

Rose: Find a Gathering.

Hillary: Yeees?

Rose: And become... Juggalettes.

(The audience knows this term, and it gets a big laugh. Hillary waits a beat, then repeats the specifics, making them MORE specific).

Hillary: Let me get this straight. You want us, two suburban mothers.

Rose: Yes.

Hillary: To get one single bottle of rosé.

Rose: Yes.

Hillary: To get in our 2006 Suburu.

Rose: The one we both share.

Hillary: Yes. And become fans of the Insane Clown Posse.

Rose screams in excitement.

> **Hillary:** Wait, you didn't hear what I have to say about it!

She then screams in excitement, and they both scream for a while. From the backline, Cody Kopp enters as another housewife.

> **Cody:** What's going on? What have I missed?

> **Hillary:** We feel alive for the first time in 20 years.

> **Cody:** You've never felt more alive!

> **Hillary:** Okay, we're going to explain this thing to you. But here's the thing with this thing: you are either all the way fucking in, or you're out, Cathy. Do you understand?

> **Cody:** Okay, what is it?

> **Rose:** Cathy, do you remember the bake-off this year?

> **Cody:** Uh-huh. I was there. Love it!

> **Rose:** You know how my brownies were flying off the table?

> **Hillary:** I am STILL working those off.

> **Cody:** Yes, me too!

> **Rose:** I was talking to my son Jerrob. His name is Jerrob. It was a compromise.

Hillary: You wanted to name him Cherub, and Hank wanted to name him Jed.

Rose: Yes.

Cody: What are you freaking out about? I was going through *Ellen* magazine and I heard screaming.

Rose: The one *Ellen* magazine that we all share?

Cody: Yes! Because $11.95 for just one person, that'd be ridiculous.

Hillary: Okay, so, we're going to buy one bottle of rosé.

Cody: Oh, I love rosé.

Hillary: We get into the Outback. We drive up the coast.

Cody: Yes.

Rose: We find a Gathering.

Hillary: We become Juggalettes.

Cody: Right.

Rose: We take angel dust all weekend. I pierce my nipples. You have sex with a GIANT man.

They all scream with delight. Scene is edited.

The specifics make the scene. Even when they digress, it is to talk about not just "a magazine," but instead an issue of *Ellen* magazine that cost $11.95.

CARE

Another way to be funny is to care more about what's happening than we would expect.

Caring is funny. Even caring just a little bit more than you expect is funny. I heard a scene between Jimmy Carrane and Michael Delaney that started with this:

> **Jimmy:** I think I'm going to have a taco salad tonight. Have you thought about what you're going to eat tonight?

> **Michael:** Yes, deeply.

Don't go too nuts or it'll feel false. Just give about 20% more of a shit than we expect you to. Err on the side of caring more than we thought you would.

Here's a scene from the improv group Convoy. Alex Berg starts a scene inspired by a statement that people become astronauts just to get access to specially-made "astronaut ice cream."

> **Berg:** Welcome to NASA's awesome ice cream bar. Would you like toppings or fold-ins today?

Todd Fasen steps up.

> **Fasen:** Just the astronaut ice cream.

> **Berg:** Man, we got like caramel sea salt, dark chocolate.

> **Fasen:** Nah, I want the astronaut ice cream.

Berg: I'll sell it to you, but that's, like, easily the least awesome ice cream we have here. It's chalky and tastes only like strawberries. The Neapolitan thing's a scam. I can give you strawberry ice cream that's rad! With wild strawberries from Peru!

Fasen: Why would I become an astronaut if I wanted a normal ice cream? If I wanted normal ice cream with fold-ins, I would have done, I don't know, any other job?

Berg: That's really harsh, man. I take a lot of pride in my work here, okay? It took a lot of funding to get the government to fund an awesome ice cream bar. One sack of strawberry ice cream. Next.

Alex Fernie walks up.

Berg: What dreams of mine can you crush today, sir?

Fernie: Do you have any recommendations?

Berg: *(moved)* Yeah! Oh my God, I have tons. Do you like waffle cones?

Fernie: Yeah, don't recommend a waffle cone. I want a kind of ice cream.

Berg: No! Yeah, I know. Oh, that's just the beginning of it! Wait, no, no, don't go away!

Fernie: You know what, no, let's forget it.

Berg: Wait, no! Sir! Hey, man! Hey! Wait!!

> **Fernie:** Nah, it's too much.

> **Berg:** No, man, no! You asked for recommendations!

> **Fernie:** You just recommended a waffle cone to me. No one walks in and says, "I want a recommendation of a waffle cone."

> **Berg:** No!!! Noooooooo!

Berg's passion powers the scene.

Find reasons to care. See this next scene between Michelle Thompson and Ruha Taslimi, where Ruha won't go to a barbecue because she doesn't want to disturb the cats that are sitting on her.

> **Ruha:** *(indicating that cats are sitting on her)* I mean I did want to go to Bob's party, but at this point I'm leaving it up to Scrambles and Mittens. They're very comfortable. If they get up, I'll go.

> **Michelle:** Ruha, come on, we RSVP'd! They're cats. Just... *(goes to push them)*

> **Ruha:** They are comfortable!

> **Michelle:** Well, they can get on their bed! They have this nice $500 freaking bed!

> **Ruha:** I love this, having cats on me. I love the way this feels more than ANYTHING.

> **Michelle:** Ruha, I have a lot riding on this barbecue. I'm new to this little pottery community, and there's a bunch of people there that I've been checking out, and I want to make some friends.

> **Ruha:** You could go!

> **Michelle:** But we're a team! You said we were a team!

Michelle's move to make the barbecue important to her keeps the scene going. She uses plausible reasons, inspired by real life, and it helps keep the scene going.

JOY

This is hard to force or express in a formula, but you should play with a sense of joy. We use the word "play" in improv deliberately. While committing and being invested and respecting the emotional truth, you should play with a sense of fun, or even mischief.

UCB co-founder Matt Walsh taught a workshop once where he kept reminding us how ephemeral improv was. "This is disposable." He kept urging us to make choices boldly and see what trouble it got us into. Our scenes became more energized and reckless.

The examples in this book were all scenes that were done with a feeling of fun and excitement. There's the sense that at any time the train could fall off the rails, and everyone is enjoying that danger.

NAME THE FUNNY THING

You've got a funny idea. Are you able to explain it? Or maybe a scene you did was actually funny, thank God, but can you describe what the funny part was? You've got to do better than just "the part where everyone screamed" or "the way Bert did the thing."

This is for when you're on the back line, watching a funny scene that you're not yet in. Use these phrases to isolate exactly what's making it work so that, maybe, you can make more of it.

Try these phrases to accurately describe what makes a scene funny:

WHAT IF: Title the game with a "what if." "What if the top clique at a high school were scientists?" (Via UCB founder Matt Walsh via UCB teacher

Alex Fernie.) That makes you isolate the main funny part.

INSTEAD OF: Say "instead of" to clarify. "A version of the show *Cops,* but instead of domestic violence and drug deals they bust people who play sex games." This forces you to say the "normal" version, which makes the "funny" part pop.

AS IF: This is direction for the performers (even if the performers are you). "A guy who tries to wow his date with a fried egg as if it were caviar or champagne." It also shows you how to play the funny part. "Play the gym trainer talking to her client as if you are a jealous girlfriend."

INITIATING WITH PREMISE

At UCB we say "initiating with a premise" to mean starting with a very full idea. We do this if we have an opening where we have already converted our suggestion into some comedy premises.

These initiations are a great way to get a scene going quickly. They're great for audiences who are very skeptical about improv or have never seen it. When you initiate with premise you are giving them the goods right away.

The other way of starting, and what most of this book has focused on, is called starting an "organic" scene. This means starting with a small idea like, "Martha, I don't think these tulips are gonna bloom!" and using yes-anding and discovery to build more slowly to a funny idea.

Premise initiations are powerful and funny, but also hard. They're often a bit wordy and ham-fisted, because you must lay out a lot of information in your first line. They require you to have the skills of a good sketch writer. You have to come up with a good idea and figure out how to word it succinctly.

The improv group Last Day of School asks audience members to read text messages from their phones to inspire scenes. At one of their shows, an audience member read this text message: "Also, spider/hormonal senses feel weird that I don't have emergency contact info for anyone close to you."

Neil Campbell started the scene as a health/sex education teacher. David Harris, Heather Campbell, and Stephanie Allyne were the students.

Neil: All right, girls, today in health class we're going to learn about getting your first period. Now you're going to start feeling things in your body. It's important to figure out if you're becoming a woman or if you're getting spider powers.

David: Is this in the textbook?

Neil: This is not in the textbook. You have to really examine what's happening with your body and understand: are you becoming a woman? Or are you becoming a web slinger?

David: When we were on the bus ride home, we went over part of a bumpy area, and I checked my underwear and there was spotting.

Neil: That sounds like getting your period. But let's make sure: were you so shocked that you leapt, and when you landed on a wall, your hands stuck to the wall?

David: No.

Neil: Sounds like you're getting your period. Probably.

Heather: I didn't even know this was a possibility.

Neil: It's a 50–50 possibility.

Heather: Okay, because I was an early bloomer and I've had my period since I was in the fourth grade. And I've been putting my tampon in during my period. Am I going to turn into a spider?

Neil: Were you fighting Doc Ock?

Heather: No, I was in the bathroom upstairs.

Neil: Okay, it sounds like you're a woman. This is good! I'm excited to clarify!

Stephanie: Well, statistics show that I'm a spider.

Neil: Have you started shooting webbing out of your wrists when you clench down here?

Stephanie: Never checked.

Neil: So it's still... either way.

Stephanie: But I damage my underwear.

Neil: Okay, how?

Stephanie: Every month, I damage my underwear, and I can't ever use it again. It undergoes intense damage.

David: Is the damage coming from a spurt of uterine lining? Or is it coming from...

Neil: ...a spider sack?

> **Stephanie:** I've never had anyone look inside of me. I just know that massive amounts of blood and clumps come out of me.

> **Neil:** Blood or webbing?

> **Stephanie:** It's hard to determine. They're clumps.

> **Neil:** Are flies attracted to it?

Then Heather tags out Neil and David and creeps like a huge spider over to Stephanie.

> **Heather:** Honey, I heard that you had your period.

> **Stephanie:** Yes.

> **Heather:** I'm so proud of you. Have you told Dad?

> **Stephanie:** No, I haven't yet.

> **Heather:** I'll do it. *(shrieks)*

David enters as another giant spider. Then Neil tags everyone out and resumes his teacher pose, and the other players become students again.

> **Neil:** Here's another question to figure out if you're becoming a woman or getting spider powers. I probably could have started with it. Are your parents giant spiders?

Advice for initiating with premise:

- **Start the moment right after the funny thing has happened.** Begin the scene with, "Attention, students. Today for dissection class I have replaced all of the frogs with kittens." This puts us in the middle of the action. Avoid "pitch" scenes where someone is proposing action for the future, like, "What if we replaced the frogs with kittens?"

- **Use phrases exactly as they were said in the opening.** If someone tells a story that going to their neighborhood feels like "going back in time" and you want to use that idea in a scene, start with, "Man, when I come to this neighborhood it feels like I've gone back in time." Don't be coy about which idea you're using.

- **End your initiation with the funny part.** Saying, "You are no longer the valedictorian. We are giving that honor to the school dolphin," is better than, "The dolphin is now going to be the valedictorian."

- **Have something.** If you're doing scenes after an opening, start with an idea. Don't start with "How's it going?" unless you are absolutely out of ideas. This happens, but make sure you know you're DOING IT WRONG.

If you're responding to the initiation:

- **Catch the inbound pass.** As described in the "Top of the Scene" section, don't do too much on the second line. Try to just say "yes" and confirm the information you're being given. It doesn't hurt to be nodding a lot as the initiator speaks.

- **Pass the fork.** If the initiation doesn't seem unusual, then just be normal and assume the initiator will get to their idea very soon. If someone says, "Hey, pass me that fork?" don't be paranoid that they're going to kill you with it or that you're being tricked. The funny part is coming later. Just pass the fork.

  Another way of saying that is: "If you don't know what the game is, don't play it."

SHOULDS

Final rule: don't worry too much about any of these rules.

Above all else, avoid doing things just because you think you should do them. That means you're bored, and the audience can tell. You must always play with the knowledge and joy of someone who is basically allowed to do whatever they want.

Rules usually have some truth in them, but still, sometimes you need to break them, just to remind them who's boss. You are a co-writer and co-director at all times during an improv scene, and you should speak your mind. Yes, it's good form to take endowments as gifts ("You always said you loved this place"), but not at the expense of removing your true, engaged self from the scene ("I have said that, but I'm realizing this is a terrible place.")

UCB teacher Andy Secunda used to do an exercise with his classes called "Silly String," using the classic product that comes in an aerosol can and sprays long, colorful strings. It's for parties, for celebrating sports team victories, and for making a mess in low-budget sketch shows. It is truly silly.

Secunda would set up a table and two chairs and place a can of Silly String on the table. Then he'd tell everyone that they were going to do scenes, two people at a time, and the only rule was that you couldn't touch or talk about the Silly String.

People would go up, two at a time, and dutifully do scenes until Secunda would call, "Edit! Two more." Sometimes everyone would go, and he would start going through the class again. He wouldn't make any comments or give any notes on the scenes.

Finally, someone would get bored and grab the Silly String and spray it. Then Secunda would stop the exercise. All rules are sometimes meant to be broken.

Our favorite improv shows are, regardless of what tone they strike or what pace they set, funny. Even if there are truly amazing and gifted acting chops on display, the part you remember when you walk out of the theater is the funny part.

BE FUNNY EXERCISES

YOU WANTED TO SEE ME?

Many of the exercises in this book are meant to produce funny scenes, but this one is meant to specifically practice creating ironic situations.

Two people in chairs. One says, "You wanted to see me, [occupation]?" where [occupation] is anything from the very general "farmer" to "head chef at the best restaurant in town."

Then the other person has to make three expected requests, and then a fourth one that is the exact opposite of what we'd expect. It should go like this:

> **Person A:** You wanted to see me, farmer?

> **Person B:** Yes, thanks. We need to order more grain, we need to get the tractor fixed, I'd like to lay off some of the hired help for budget reasons, and also I'd like us to stop growing food.

Then Person A "straight mans" it, meaning they try to respond like a rational person would.

> **A:** Uh, but all we do is grow food. We're a farm.

Person B then has to come up with a reason why they want to do the weird thing. For the purposes of this exercise, it doesn't even matter if they have a good reason. We're getting used to having an ironic agenda.

The straight man should ask why, and then the person with the occupation should come up with a reason why. Again, don't worry about this too much. Although there are a lot of exercises that focus on the why, this one is actually more about enjoying it when there's someone behaving in the exact opposite way from how we expect.

It shouldn't be random. This wouldn't be as good:

> **A:** You wanted to see me, farmer?

> **B:** Yes, thanks. We need to order more grain, we need to get the tractor fixed, I'd like to lay off some of the hired help for budget reasons, and also I'd like a pet dolphin living in my house.

That's kind of funny, but it's sloppy.

Once you've done a few, you can broaden the occupation to be a short description of a character. Like this:

> **A:** You wanted to see me, guy going through a hostile divorce?

> **B:** Yes, come in. I'd like to make an appointment with my lawyer. I'd also like to set up some therapy for myself. Call my friends to see who wants to hang out with me for a drink. And then hire a poet to write a love sonnet about my marriage.

Choosing the opposite of what you'd expect from someone reveals what you think the most important and defining aspect of that someone is. I saw a "You wanted to see me?" like this:

> **A:** You wanted to see me, Stevie Wonder?

> **B:** *(not worrying about doing a vocal impersonation, by the way)* Yes, sit down. I'd like to have my piano cleaned for the upcoming concert. Let's call the venue to make sure everything is in order. I'd like to hire some different session musicians to rehearse with. And then I want to start painting.

This person was seizing on the fact that Stevie Wonder is blind. That can work—it is well-known that Stevie is blind.

But is that Stevie Wonder's primary quality? Is he known primarily for being someone who is blind, in the way that, say, Louis Braille or Helen Keller was? No, he's known primarily for being a musician.

The student tried again and did this:

> **B:** Okay, have my piano cleaned. Let's get some studio time soon. I'd like a new tour manager. And then I'd like to talk to someone about getting my hands removed.

> **A:** But you're a musician! You need your hands to play the piano, or anything!

> **B:** Come on! People were impressed that I could be a recording star while being blind—think how impressed they'll be when I do it without hands!

It was better. This isn't meant to be a lecture on sensitivity. It's pointing out the importance of being precise, or at least, highlighting that the way you choose to make something ironic reveals what you think the most important aspect of something is.

THE SAMURAI

Practicing being funny is tough. Here's an exercise designed to reward you when you do something that is both funny and still productive for an improv scene.

4–6 people up on the back line. They are the "samurai." They will be doing the scenes.

Another 4–6 people along the side walls. They are the "sensei." The sensei will only be watching the improv, not doing it. ("Sensei" isn't the historically accurate term, but I find it more palatable than "master" and also more cool to say.)

Give each of the sensei five playing cards and assign to them one of the samurai.

If Erik is one of the samurai on the back line, you assign Gwen, who is on the side line and holding five playing cards, to be his sensei.

The samurai get a suggestion and do an improv set. Normal improv set: they edit, they tag-out, they do walk-ons.

But before they start, you give the samurai a mission (examples below). They can all have the same one or maybe they have separate ones. Whenever a samurai accomplishes their mission, their sensei steps out right then and hands them a card.

Sensei should err on the side of being generous.

Keep going until all cards have gone out.

FIRST ROUND: ACCEPT OFFERS
First time I do this, all the samurai have the same mission: ACCEPT OFFERS. Every time they explicitly yes-and something that was just said, their sensei steps out and gives them a card.

If Sam says to Erik, "Sergeant, I'm exhausted," and Erik says, "You look exhausted," then Erik's sensei Gwen steps forward right then and hands him a card.

Then if Erik keeps going and says, "You should be, having been on watch all night," and Sam says, "I was out there, but I'm not sure I did a great job," then Sam gets a card because he's acknowledging he was on watch.

It gets tricky/helpful/funny when people make accusations and the recipient has to make them true.

If Arnie steps out and says, "Clarissa, you jerk!" and then Clarissa goes "Shut up, asshole!" Clarissa would get a card.

It is somewhat subjective what merits a card. The teacher should confirm or deny the first few times cards are given out ("Yep, that's right," or "No, he's not confirming anything," or even "Where's the card on that?"), but then try to back off.

Once the cards are all out, switch sensei and samurai.

SECOND ROUND: SPECIFIC MISSIONS

Once everyone's had a chance to do the "accept offers" round, do one where each samurai has separate tasks.

FUN TASKS TO ASSIGN:

- **Emotional reaction:** Get a card whenever you make a pronounced emotional reaction.

- **Toys:** When someone uses an object that you created, you get a card.

- **Specificity:** Whenever you are surprisingly specific, you get a card.

- **Made-up proper nouns:** Any time you make a specific reference to something that is made up ("You guys seen the new Jules Candy film?"), you get a card.

- **Justification:** Any time you explain something that was contradictory, you get a card

- **Playing against type:** Any time you play someone who is not your gender/age/general energy, you get a card.

You can still give "accept offers" as a mission here, too.

These missions are supposed to be easy, fun things that an audience enjoys. They're not heady logical things like "playing game" or "taking an idea from the opening." They are things that the audience likes the moment they happen and that generally enrich a scene.

THIRD ROUND: GROUP MISSIONS

In addition to the sensei who are up on the side walls, you can assign students watching to be sensei, looking for missions that anyone in the group can accomplish. These are optional missions that are not any one samurai's responsibility, and some are accomplished by the group together, as a whole.

When the group sensei see their mission accomplished, they should throw a playing card in the air and shout the name of the mission, to indicate it was just accomplished. Some group missions are:

- **Stage picture:** Whenever the group strikes a good stage picture, this sensei throws a card in the air and declares, "Stage picture!"

- **Truthful moment:** Whenever someone in the group says something that is surprisingly truthful, this sensei throws a card in the air and says, "Truthful moment!"

- **Moment of silence:** There's so much frantic talking in improv that an audience appreciates committed silence. Whenever there's a nice, pregnant moment of pause, this sensei throws a card in air and says, "Moment of silence!" (This ironically both celebrates and ruins it.)

- **True love:** Improv also has so much scattershot meanness and snarkiness that any time there's a moment of genuine vulnerable sweetness—someone saying "I love you," a father complimenting his son, a friend helping a friend—this sensei throws a card in the air and says, "True love!"

These missions don't all have to be completed—meaning these sensei don't need to get rid of all their cards for the round to be over. It would take too long.

This can be a chaotic exercise, but if you build up from the first, simple "accept offers" version, it can be a fun celebration of the types of moments that make improv shows fun.

The sensei are watching more closely than they are maybe used to.

The samurai focus their awareness down to just one useful task.

The businesslike action of handing a card to someone is an oddly pleasing punchline for otherwise mundane improv moments.

It rewards being fun and funny.

BE HEALTHY

CHILL THE FUCK OUT

I relate to people who feel obsessed with improv comedy. I have been and continue to be obsessed with it. Ironically, in order to really get good at improv, and in order to stay emotionally healthy while we do it, we have to follow a piece of advice that contradicts all of that.

I once interviewed UCB teacher and performer Chris Gethard about what he teaches when he teaches improv. Chris is the best improv teacher I have ever known. Students who took his classes—which was everyone in the early days of the UCB Theatre—would consistently swear that it was in a Chris Gethard class where they figured improv out and found their own comedic voice. Naturally, I was very excited to hear Chris's take on what he teaches.

His very first piece of advice: "Chill the fuck out."

I think he was mostly talking about being calm and having poise at the top of a scene. Don't over-react to things and make a big deal about nothing, just because you're impatient for things to happen.

But it's pretty good advice for your overall improv approach, especially under the banner of "Be Healthy."

We improv nerds have to chill the fuck out.

In order to get better, you must let go a bit. Get some perspective. Realize that "say yes" is really only useful in the beginning of a scene, and that once you realize the point of the scene—the game, the funny part—saying yes isn't really a priority anymore.

Realize that "follow the fear" speaks mainly to a general attitude of bravery on the part of the actor, and that for the characters in a scene it's almost completely irrelevant how brave they are being. Realize that not every improv exercise is good.

Realize that your improv teachers may be good actors and writers, but they are not trying nor are they able to fix your life. They are often as weird as you, but to make it worse they have their status in an improv community—very high within the bubble of the community, but mostly imaginary to the rest of the world—gumming up their radar of what to do in their lives.

Realize that an improv audition is not a referendum on you as a person and that an improv theater's rejection of you means almost nothing.

Sometimes improv seems like a grand religion. It can be inspiring and overwhelming, and there's a lot to learn when you see improv like that. But other times it's just a set of best practices for brainstorming together on stage. It's a relief to remember that. Let improv be small: a handful of guidelines for working together to make some funny things.

Value real friends over status. Don't drink too much too often. Avoid toxic people and groups. Take breaks. Miss things now and then—the show everyone says you *have* to watch, the workshop everyone's dying to get into, even your own show—so you can re-charge. If your friend is getting married during the weekend of auditions for house teams, skip the audition.

Letting go of improv and taking it off of its pedestal is part of getting good at it.

YOU WILL NEVER FIGURE THIS OUT

I mean this as a consolation: you will never completely figure out improv. Not forever, anyhow. You'll have a grasp on it for a few weeks, maybe even a few months, and then it moves away from you. You stumble upon a new exercise or a new mantra and can do no wrong. It gives you decisive moves and confident viewpoints. Audiences like you right away.

Then it fades, and you are lost again, searching for the next key.

Here are several things that have given me the key to being good at improv in the past:

- "listen and react"
- "find the game"
- "match energy"
- "accept every offer"
- "live life onstage"
- "justify"
- "point of view"
- "be brave and honest"
- "chill out"

Each one of those was like a booster rocket for a while, and then each one weirdly stopped working. I had to switch up my game and try something else.

It's as if improv is this invisible balloon that you cannot get your arms all the way around, no matter what. You hold it, just barely, but then it gives and starts to slip away, so you must adjust your arms and find your grip again.

YOU MUST APPRECIATE THE GOOD IN WHAT YOU DO

A big sub-category of "be healthy" is "be kind to yourself."

Beating yourself up is easy and natural for an improviser, but you must learn to see the good in the scenes you do and hold onto it. It is both an essential tool of getting better and an emotional survival skill.

You will do many scenes like the following.

Suggestion: "dartboard." Already, you're panicking. *Should I just play darts? Is that too obvious?* No, you decide, it's okay that you're just in a bar. *Okay, I'm playing darts in a bar.* Phew, decided. *Oh my god, I've been standing here for too long. Quick, start playing darts.* You throw an imaginary dart, fast, and set up to throw another one, and you think: *I'm playing darts.*

Scene partner enters, and he's smoking a cigarette and taking a drag every two seconds. You think you have to say you're playing darts so he knows, so you say, "I'm playing darts." Before you're even done saying that, though, he says, "Aren't you supposed to be bartending?" and the other people in your class laugh. You want to say "yes" because that's what improv is, so you say, "Yes, I'm bartending, but first I'm playing darts. Would you like to play darts? Come on, play darts!" Now your scene partner has started to play darts with you, and three seconds that feel like three hours go by, and then you say, "Good dart game."

Then he goes, "You know what? We suck at darts," and maybe one person watching laughs, and it's a relief. But part of your brain says *wait, no, that's a denial,* and then before you know it you say, "I'm fucking your wife," and your partner, who has been noted for fighting too much, goes, "Hey, man, it's cool. I don't care about her. Let's just play darts!" And the teacher says, "Okay, two more, notes later."

And you won't remember the notes because your brain is full of this: "I am terrible."

Bad scene? Oh, yeah. For sure. But also, you actually did a lot correctly. Can you see it?

- You got a suggestion and made a clear who/what/where.
- You interacted with a scene partner, and you agreed with each other's reality.
- You each said yes to the other at least once.
- You avoided a dumb fight.
- You made decisions even though you weren't sure.
- You agreed on a history.

You got up out of your normal life and came to an improv class and got up in front of people and were brave and vulnerable. You put yourself out there. Your brain has started to blaze new trails within itself of making choices, and those trails will be quicker to travel next time.

You did improv.

You must appreciate the good in what you do. No one else will ever pay as much attention to you as you will, so learn to be a genuine but generous audience for yourself.

You are good. You wouldn't have wanted to do this so badly if it wasn't a good fit for your brain. Keep going.

HOW DO I GET OUT OF MY HEAD?

One of the main consequences of being kind to yourself is that you will get out of your own head.

Getting out of your head refers to the desire to be doing improv without having your head full of rules and thoughts and worries. It means you want to just play, rather than be paralyzed by all the rules your improv teachers have told you. You want to stop feeling stuck on stage, like you've lost your instinct of what to do next, and you want to stop doubting yourself and worrying constantly. You feel this way and you're tired of it—what can you do?

Closely related to this question is: "I just had a terrible class/practice/show, and now I'm in a rut. What should I do?"

The best advice I've heard isn't mine. It's from UCB performer Zach Woods, in an email he sent to then-UCB student (now teacher and performer) Achilles Stamatelaky about this very problem. In Achilles' words:

> In May 2006, I had no confidence in my improv. After taking classes for a year-and-a-half, I felt like I was only getting worse at performing. I sent the following e-mail to some of the teachers and coaches I'd worked closely with at the time to seek their advice.
>
> *I'm not feeling great about my improv and I hope you can give me some advice.*
>
> *I don't remember when I've felt this unconfident in my performance. For*

the past month or so, I've constantly felt indecisive in scenes (both in practices and performances). I also feel way in my head and tentative. I find myself making moves because they seem like the "right" move to make, not because they're best for the scene or the most fun. I'm making weak choices and end up in mediocre scenes because of it. In other words, I feel like I'm stuck "improvising" rather than "playing" a scene.

Part of my lack of confidence might stem from having some really great rehearsals and shows in March, then having really high expectations of myself in April during Harold team auditions and not meeting those expectations. That I got rejected from two teacher-approved performance workshops hasn't helped my confidence either. It's a vicious cycle.

What do you do when you feel like you're in a rut? I want to feel like I'm improving my skills as an improviser in some way, but I haven't felt confident in weeks. I don't see myself getting out of this slump anytime soon.

Thanks again for all your help.

—Achilles

Zach responded with the following.

Hey Achilles,

I'm sorry you're feeling this way. Everyone gets in ruts from time to time, and I know how discouraging it feels. While there are some things you can do to help, I think the short (and probably disappointing) answer is you've just got to ride it out. Ruts always last longer than we want them to, but they don't last forever. So try to be patient... as impossible as that sounds.

Here's some other stuff...

- I think sometimes people who care a great deal about improv can get so wrapped up in the improv community and improv itself that their self-esteem becomes dependent on the quality of their improv. This happens to me more often than I'd like, and it's always bad news for both my improv and my self-esteem. I think it's important to remember (especially when you're in a slump) that the qualities that make you valuable as a human being have nothing to do with group games or tag-outs. Whether or not you're a worthwhile person has nothing to do with improv. If you're doing awesome shows, you could still be an asshole, if you're doing bad shows

you could still be a kind, generous guy. Hopefully you're not neurotic enough to be plagued by these issues, but, I know I am, so I figured I'd mention this stuff, just in case. So...

Remind yourself that your value as a person is in no way related to, or dependent on the quality of your improv.

- Another thing that can put people in their heads is a need to "achieve."

While it's great to get some validation in the form of recognition or approval, I think it's best not to put too much stock in external recognition. The warm, mushy feeling that comes from 'achieving' (getting put on a team, class, etc.) is fleeting, and soon you're back to worrying and working and trying to improve. I think it's good to be patient and to move at your own rate. Try not to measure your progress against other people's progress. I know that's hard (maybe impossible) but I think if you allow yourself to improve at your own rate, it liberates you from the self-conscious, inse- cure, self-flagellation that is anathema to good improv. Put your nose to the grindstone and do the work. It's important to have goals, but I think it's also important that those goals be rooted in personal progress rather than external achievement.

- Slumps are sometimes a result of improv-overkill. If you've been watch- ing and doing improv constantly, it's possible that you're a bit burnt out. Good improv isn't inspired by other improv, it's inspired by life. If all you do is do/watch improv, you may have a deficit of life experiences to draw from. Take time to do the non-improv activities that you enjoy— things that have absolutely nothing to do with comedy. This will allow you to recharge. It will also put you back in touch with the things that make you unique and interesting as a person. That stuff is essential to good improv. Improv isn't just about game and technique, it's also about personality. It's important to take time to do non-comedy things that make you who you are. Listen to the music you like, read a book, fly a kite, hang out with your non-improv friends, go swimming, walk a dog, do whatever you want as long as it doesn't require a coach. Just get away from improv.

In a weird way it's kind of like the game of a scene. If all you do in a scene is hit game, game, game, and you never play the reality of the scene, both the game and the scene will feel inorganic and contrived. Similarly, in life, if all you do is improv, improv, improv, and you don't do interesting, fun non-improv stuff, your improv will feel stiff, and your life won't feel so good either (in my experience).

- Get a new pair of shoes. I don't know if this works, but I was in a slump once and I asked Peter Gwinn what I should do. He told me to get new shoes and wear them during rehearsals/shows. Make sure they are significantly different from the shoes you currently wear to rehearsals/performances. This might be bullshit, but it might be a miracle cure.

- Eat healthy, sleep well, exercise. I find that this stuff makes a huge difference. Taking care of your body allows you to focus better, etc. You probably already do this, but if not, eat some soy and get 8 hours of REM.

- If you feel like a show/rehearsal went badly, don't beat yourself up. If you notice yourself moping or obsessing over the show, try to do something to take your mind off it. You are not helping your improv by mentally abusing yourself. Self-flagellation is just a way of indulging one's own insecurities and fears. Sometimes you can't help it, but try to avoid abusing yourself if you can.

- And remember, your slump is temporary. It's more in your own head than in reality.

Be patient, relax, and your slump will pass. Seriously.

You're going to be alright,

Zach

PS. I apologize if this email comes off as pedantic and/or convoluted.

Besides the great advice, my favorite part of this email is that Zach apologizes at the end for having written it.

DON'T QUIT BECAUSE OF A RUT

Ruts happen to everyone. Some time ago, after a show, I wrote this down in a note to myself:

I don't want to do it anymore. I know I'll change my mind soon, maybe even after a single night's sleep but I want to capture what this feels like.

Did the show tonight and my goal going in was to be less ego-driven. Less concerned about how I was doing, how funny I was—because that makes my defenses go up and makes me mean for no good reason and makes me defensive. I wanted to just be in the moments and feel them and be confident and playful.

In a sense I was successful—I did not feel angry or defensive. I enjoyed the show. But I also felt toothless and out of ideas. Uninspired. Does one have to go with the other—serenity and an empty head? The Buddhists would say yes. But are Buddhists funny?

I could quit tonight. I could be done. I've had a blessed improv career and I could just stop and not perform again and focus on writing and maybe computer programming and who knows. Like maybe I've used up my last good idea.

Man, I felt like a fraud a bunch tonight. Just with no idea of what to do or say, or what could be funny. How did I get on this team? It feels like weeks since I've been in a groove there. I'm just someone who's good at obeying a system, it's why I succeeded at a hierarchal improv theatre rather than in the wilds of stand-up, scripted acting, etc. Learn enough people's names and they'll put you on a team.

My teammates were good. I enjoyed watching them. I felt like a pillar of NO or else a brainless arbitrary scattershot of nice. Couldn't commit.

But YES, I was serene! Really! I wasn't panicking or going into dumb rants or attacking people for no reason. I had philosophies, I could see the room around me my characters were in. I must remember that: I accomplished my goal.

Doesn't matter. I feel done.

When I feel like I did that night, I often think of times that I've heard people who I think are great express their doubt in themselves. I think, "This person is crazy—they're really good! They have some weird self-defeating thing going on that they're giving into." When I think of that, then I can more easily cast off my own self-defeatism.

Someone else would look at me and think *I'm* crazy for feeling discouraged, so I put this here to make *you* forget your own self-defeatism. It happens to everyone; it's mostly pointless.

A separate thing I remember is all the people who quit before me. I've run into people I took classes with, and they say, "Yeah, sometimes I wish I'd stuck with it. I saw you in that show and remember how we were in class…" and I think, "Thank God I didn't quit."

I remember that, and then I don't quit. I shake it off. The universe will kick me out of this game when it's time for me to go.

HOW SHOULD I APPROACH MY IMPROV AUDITION?

You have an audition coming up and you're obsessing about it. Or maybe you just had one and didn't get cast and you're obsessing about that. How should you handle these things? Here are my best pieces of advice.

First, know that all audition and casting processes are strange animals. I can't think of a better way to do it, but it's also not a perfect system. You'd like to think that an audition process is like an improv computer that takes in all the available data about the people auditioning: how good they are in classes, how positive their attitude is, how well they treat their teammates, how much they've gotten better, how well they've taken notes from their teachers, how many improv books and blogs they read, how much they care, how much respect they garner from their peers, etc.

Nope. The people running the auditions will not know most of that information. They're going to watch your audition, and based on their experience watching improv, make a guess at how good you are at it.

I've been in the room on the casting side for several improv auditions. The people running them have genuine intentions of getting the best people. They have been on the other side of the audition table, they are sympathetic, and they care.

But emotions run high. Sometimes people have preconceived opinions of performers that are tough to shake. A surprisingly great scene can become a story that everyone roots for, beyond the actual abilities of the people in it. A good person will come through at a time when everyone watching is exhausted. The person who would have lobbied for you has already lobbied for too many people that day and has no more lobbying clout by the time you walk in the room. It's easy to overlook subtle, quiet players. Running auditions and making good decisions is hard!

When you're watching dozens, even hundreds, of people audition for an improv team, it feels like this: about 10% are undeniably very strong, about 10% are definitely not ready, and the other 80% are fine.

They're fine. They follow the rules, and they have decent chops. They do an audition that is solid but not spectacular. The various people watching the audition don't have that much time to sort it out, and it ends up being a little bit of a crapshoot in terms of who in the 80% gets regarded as good enough.

One way to do well in your audition, of course, is to be in that top 10%. Be undeniably, consistently, very good.

What about the other 80%? How can you put your best self forward, and stand out as much as possible?

Make sure that when you do improv, you are connected to your own internal sense of what is good. Improvise how you want to. Sure, there are principles and techniques that you've been taught. But which ones really work for you? If you pay attention to your own taste and perform according to your own standards, you will be playing with confidence. Confidence is funny. It takes practice to figure out what you like, but once you pay attention you will know.

Don't try to perform the way you think your teacher wants you to. If you do that, you'll be playing in order to "do it right." That's not bad to do when you're in a class and learning something new, but on stage you have to be showing the audience what you think. When someone is auditioning to please someone else, it feels false. It just doesn't work. You must be yourself, which takes practice.

Another thing that helps: perform with the best people you can. Performing with good people may be more valuable than anything else, including having great teachers. You will absorb their pace, their standards, their energy. Being on stage with good people keeps you present, because you will be genuinely absorbed in what they do and have to say. Nothing makes you a better actor than being truly interested in seeing what's coming.

I've written earlier about the strength you get from being willing to play with people you consider difficult. That's more about avoiding a judgmental headspace that will get in the way of your performance. For quickly increasing your improv skills, get with good people when you can.

On stage, practice always taking the high road. This is related to the "Be Brave" mentality. When in doubt during a set: say yes, care more, be emotionally vulnerable, go with your friend's idea, react, put yourself out there. You know the fundamentals: do them. Take the high road, every time there is a doubt. If the show goes badly, you'll want to know that you committed, you said yes, you were brave.

Get used to doing your part the best you can, to your own satisfaction, every time. People will notice that you are performing as a confident, self-sustaining agent. You will be interesting and your best self this way. This will translate in an audition setting.

Here's what doesn't matter: "playing politics." Things like interning at the theater, going to the right parties, becoming friends with teachers, becoming a tech and running lights, or going to a million shows and sitting in the front row so everyone sees that you're seeing shows. None of that will significantly help you have a good audition.

I've heard many people say that auditioners put their friends on, but I've been in the rooms and they don't. In one house team audition I saw a real, professional casting director—who had hired some of the auditioners for acting jobs—and he didn't make the cut. "He's not ready," said someone in evaluating his performance.

If someone who can hire the auditioners for actual acting jobs can't get on a team, going to the right parties isn't going to help you.

Instead of playing politics, do the things in the community that genuinely interest you. If interning gets you free classes and you like classes, do it. If you think a party is going to be fun, go to that party. If you naturally become friends with the senior performers and teachers, and you just like those people, then let those friendships flower forth naturally. If you enjoy the shows, go to the shows. In these ways, you will be becoming your real self in the community.

But if you're doing things "to get on a team," don't bother. It won't help. You will get trumped by someone doing better improv.

Now what if you don't get cast?

First of all, please do not immediately write a check for another class. Lots of improv theaters require you to take classes in order to improvise. That's the economic reality: many improv theaters keep the shows very cheap and instead make money off their schools. If we think of the theater as part of the training ground of the school, almost like an apprenticeship, then I can get behind it.

But when students keep throwing tons of money at classes to have repeated attempts at auditioning for the house teams at that theater, I feel that they are pursuing what amounts to a toxic relationship.

If you don't get cast and the only way to try again is to take another class, ask yourself: are you excited about that class for its own sake? Are you still excited about training to do improv? Can you afford it? Is there a way to get a free class, like with a scholarship or an internship? Is there a teacher you're genuinely excited to study with, which you would do regardless of whether or not it might give you an audition? Will you be glad you took this class if you don't get cast on a team, which, if you didn't get on the first time, is the statistical probability?

If the answer to questions like these is yes, then by all means take that class. Enjoy it. And go for the audition that it lets you have with enthusiasm.

I got on a house team after four classes. Then, even while I was on a team, I took sixteen more. I had a day job that paid me well, and I simply loved improv classes. I wasn't going into those classes with an agenda of getting on a team. I was going into them because I liked the learning experiences they gave me.

If you're paying for an audition opportunity, and that's really all you're doing, and you're not wealthy, then it might be time to let go of your desire to be on a team.

There's a ton of status and attention that goes with being on a house team. It's exciting. I have loved it and continue to love it. You can't take classes at a theater without at least wanting to be on their house teams.

But wanting to be on a team can also really screw with your head. It's not worth feeling bad about yourself or spending money unnecessarily. Improv should be fun and nurturing. If it's not, get away from it.

I heard a great teacher tell a class: "If your only goal in comedy is to get on a house team at an improv theater, then have a bigger goal."

FOXHOLE PEOPLE

Improv is full of comedians. Comedians are by their nature critics and cynics and skeptics. And yet, despite that, there are comedians who have positive, encouraging, supportive natures. These are the people you want in the foxhole with you when you go into (comedy) battle. Find these people, be around them, and be one of them.

One of the signs of these foxhole people is that they find positive stories in the world around them. They do it reflexively.

My friend Phil Jackson is an improviser and one of these people. I know this because one night we were out, and I was telling him that I had gotten some bad news: a script I had submitted to a network had been rejected. He looked at me and said, "That's too bad, but it's also good because..." and he trailed off for a second before saying, "...you met people. You've got contacts."

He had decided there was something good *before he had decided what was good.* He assumed there was a silver lining, and then found it. His brain was reaching for the good before he even knew for sure it was there. He was doing that for me, his friend, to help me feel better.

I walked away from that conversation thinking, "That's how to be: assume there's a good story somewhere, and just grab for it."

Foxhole person.

Another one of my friends is Lauren Lapkus, who is one of the funniest people I have ever met. When you do a show with Lauren, it is she who is glad to see you. She says hi, and she is excited you're doing the show. After the show, no matter how it goes, she tells you that you did great. She says, "You are so funny." And even if you know that's kind of not true on that particular night, you're glad she told you. It matters. You never feel like you've let her down.

Foxhole person.

These are the people who remember to ask you about you, who remember your good moves and your good shows when you're in a rut, who don't blame you when the show is bad, even when you made the bad moves.

They also pay their dues on time. They help clean up after parties. They tend not to talk trash in online discussions. They step out when your scene is dying and get right in there and commit to it with you.

No one's perfect. We all have our days when we just don't have enough energy to be a foxhole person. But the more you're around these people, the more you'll be like them. And then you will be a foxhole person for someone else.

FRIEND TEAM

Have a Friend Team. This is a team of people that you play with just because you like them as human beings. You all love improv, sure, but you also just love each other. You don't have to be good. You just have to feel comfortable with them.

This is the reward you get for being willing to play with "that guy," as described in the "Difficult People" section. You also get to pick your favorite people—not necessarily your favorite improvisers, but your favorite people—and do improv with them.

A Friend Team is where you feel like yourself, where you are relaxed. Where everyone is just cool to each other.

Sometimes, Friend Teams are also Great Teams. If that happens, never let go.

TEAM MEETINGS

At the UCB Theatre, all teams have coaches. It is taboo to discuss a show with your team without a coach present. But not every community is big enough to have the luxury of coaches. Even in a big community, sometimes you'll do a show your coach didn't come to. But for some reason or another, every team will invariably discuss a show amongst itself immediately after finishing, with no one there to mediate.

What if you think there is a problem on your team? Or you want to address the kinds of shows you're having? That means you're going to have a team meeting.

Team meetings can be tricky. When you are on a team, your view of that team is distorted. It's very hard to know exactly how a show is really coming off. Emotions can run high, especially right after shows, and it's very easy for people to take things personally.

But it's your team, and you—and everyone else on it—has a right to be heard.

Here's some general advice for team meetings.

Don't say too much right after a show. Right after a show is a fragile time. Some people automatically get critical, others very sensitive. Wait until another day.

Sit on impulses, especially angry ones. If you are thinking that you have the answer to your group's problems, or that you know that this one person is the whole problem, wait for a show or two. Do you still think that? Those thoughts often pass.

Make sure you've taken the note you want to give. I can't tell you how many times I've witnessed this: that the person who is the most upset about a certain improv crime is the one doing the crime the most. The person who insists that the team must play it real is the first one to make it cartoony in a show. The person who wants big decisions often will not make any decisions. Before you get annoyed at a certain behavior, ask yourself if you're guilty of it.

Don't do it over email. Tone is confusing over email. It's so easy to read into messages and find something there that's not there. If you must have a group discussion over email, be brief and direct. Huge long swaths of text that are meant to be diplomatic just muddle the message and can even come off as indulgent. Rather than, "I know that what I'm about to say applies as much to me as anyone, and of course I'm very open…" or "This is coming from having done dozens and dozens of shows…" just say, "I think we're jumping on the first idea too quickly."

Watch a tape of the show together. It is a harrowing experience to watch yourself and your team on tape, but it's also illuminating. You will appreciate how quiet you are as a performer or how much you're slouching. Never again will you enter onto the stage doing crazy karate chops or dancing and clapping. The thing you thought got a huge laugh didn't really. On the other hand, the part of the show you remember as being excruciating actually went pretty well.

Be honest. Think of how you describe your feelings to your best friend who is not in your improv group. Are you as direct with the people in your improv group? Would they be surprised to hear what you think?

Offer a specific constraint. Rather than use a hard-to-interpret directive like "let's be more grounded" use a specific, easy-to-follow constraint. Some examples: no tag-outs in the first three scenes. Don't heighten the first unusual thing. No starting scenes in chairs. A beat of silence at the top of scenes. Or no silence at the top of scenes. A different opening. A different form.

Finally, ask yourself: **Is the show working?** This is a tricky one: are you sure there *is* a problem? Just because it's not going how you want doesn't mean it's wrong. Are you trying to be the group's director from within the group? Improv doesn't work so well like that. If you're regularly struggling with this, it might be time to move over to sketch, where you can write a script for actors to do what you want, which is not a bad thing to realize if that's where you are.

Here's some advice from other improvisers on how they talk with their teams.

> "How do I deal with something my team does that I don't like? Answer: I turn that question around into a more positive question: What do I want my team to do *instead of that*? I answer that question, and then recommend in practice that we make an effort to do that thing. I find it works! And you usually don't end up starting arguments or sowing the seeds of discontent."

> "My team (of all women—this doesn't matter, but it might in terms of communication) used to be very negative after shows we didn't like but we found that it really wasn't helpful. We couldn't go back and change it and group negativity kind of sucks. So now we make a conscious effort to not be negative, and we don't really discuss our shows after at all, which is way better for us. Occasionally, we have our coach come note a show and then discuss it in the next practice rather than right after. I think not focusing on negativity works really well for us."

"We have a team meeting every six months or so where we reevaluate goals/talk about forms/coaches, etc. We try to regularly remember that this is supposed to be a fun thing we get to do with our friends so let's keep it fun (while still working to improve)! I think that improv lesson of 'treating your teammates like they're scholars and poets' is really important off stage too for successful team communication! I try to value my teammates' opinions as much if not more than my own, and I think that helps everyone listen and appreciate each other's input."

"If you have a regular coach, discuss the idea or concern you have with them first; that is part of a coach's duty to a team they coach regularly. They weigh the idea and maybe even broach the topic in practice. When you talk to the team, start with a positive you have about the group, so they know from the beginning that you're not attacking or criticizing. Say what you want, not what you don't want. Ask for others' opinions on the idea. End with another positive."

"... really, the keys to good team communication are the same things that are key in good scene work: listen actively, communicate what you want, support the shit out of each other, and if you're not having fun, step back and figure out why not."

"We set up dinner meetings at least once a month to talk about how we're feeling in general as a group & what our goals are. I had to leave a previous team because they were a lot of closed-off dudes who could not talk about real feelings."

"I use a lot of 'I feel'—'I feel this opening isn't playing to our strengths' or 'I feel like we could work on grounding our second beats more.' I also try to focus on the stuff I need to work on, not going too negative."

"The most successful talks I've been part of are 'what worked?' talks. 'I loved when you did that tag out run in the second beat' kind of stuff. That way we know what people dig, and can try and repeat the fun and successful moves in the next show."

Remember, you ultimately cannot control other people. If you're only going to be happy if other people do certain things, you will never be happy in your improv shows. Improv is about being surprised and reacting to it. If people are listening and not denying the facts of what you are saying, there's not much room to complain.

The best teams I've been on are full of people who are capable of taking care of themselves.

DON'T DRINK TOO MUCH

Technically this is beyond the scope of this book, but I want to point out that for many people who do improv for a long time, there may be a phase where they drink too much and go out too much. Many people also then consciously go through a phase where they cut back on that.

Improv is largely a young person's game. Lots of people do it in college and then right after college, so improv communities tend to be made up of lots of people in their mid-20s. These people like going out and often like drinking a bunch. "Partying," as people like to say.

It's also an artist's life. Lots of people who do improv also tend to pick lifestyles that keep them out of cubicles and office jobs, meaning they don't need to get up earlier in the morning. Not everyone, but lots.

There is a good side to all this, where people who don't want to live a square's life can be with like-minded people and enjoy their lives. Improv attracts the counter-culture, which is great.

But there is a bad side, where some people can almost freeze themselves in place with some bad habits. Adult children and cases of arrested development abound.

Everyone is different, so your mileage may vary, and this may not be a big deal at all for you.

My own personal experience was that I let that go for too long. At the age of 42, I was still staying out with people who were 25 until far too late, drinking too much, and acquiring an increasingly negative, bitter attitude as I did it.

I had to consciously switch up my habits, which I found not easy. I had to prioritize it and buckle down on acquiring some good emotional habits. Once I did, I felt better and healthier, and I was glad I did. I noticed that many of my peers had already kind of done that on their own, simply heading home after shows.

I'm writing this here for the younger version of myself: there's nothing wrong with going out and tying one on with your friends, but be aware that you may reach a point where this isn't a good fit for you and you'd rather just go home after your show. If you're realizing that, go ahead and let that happen. You're not missing anything.

This all goes triple if you live in New York City, where the bars never close and no one has to drive.

EXERCISES FOR BEING HEALTHY

Try these exercises for your next improv practice.

EXERCISE:
HAVE RICHER SOURCE MATERIAL

1. Two people up.

2. Leave the practice and go see a movie.

3. Talk about it together afterwards at a coffee shop.

Alternate versions: read a book, see a play, go to a concert. Something neither of you has seen or heard.

EXERCISE:
BETTER LISTENING

1. One person up.

2. Leave the practice and find a friend or acquaintance and get into a conversation.

3. See how little you can say without the person noticing.

Tips: Whenever you are asked a question, answer it quickly and then immediately ask it back to the person. Ask what they did that day (better than the more open ended "How's it going?" which is harder to answer). Complain about social media.

THOUGHTS ON CONVENTIONS AND FORMS

I'm going to offer some thoughts and advice on various improv forms, but in order to save space, I am not going to explain what the various forms actually are. If you want to know about the forms I refer to here, I suggest *The Upright Citizens Brigade Comedy Improvisation Manual,* or a service I discovered called "The Internet."

CONVENTIONS

Getting the Suggestion
Whoever gets it should repeat it so the whole audience and team can hear. Then thank the person who gave it to you. "I heard 'bread knife.' Thank you."

Tricky Suggestions
If it's a blue suggestion, like a dirty word or a suggestive object, use A-to-C to get away from the most obvious meaning but still have some relation to the spirit of the term. If you get "dildo," then do a scene about a factory worker being replaced by a machine. The first line should make the A-to-C connection clear, like, "So you're replacing me in the factory with a machine? A machine can do my job better than me?"

When you get a suggestion that is the juicy tabloid subject of the moment, try to address the spirit of the story without making yourself do celebrity impersonations. If it's a celebrity sex scandal, make it about a sex scandal among some normal folk. Ideally, you won't be totally copping out, but you also avoid trapping yourself into doing a tired, bad job of very obvious jokes.

If one of your teammates just jumps on the grenade and actually does the most obvious, troublesome meaning of a tough suggestion, get in there and commit your way through it.

The most impressive handling of a tricky suggestion I saw was from a show called "Tracers." Their show always consisted of scenes in and around a single location. At one show, someone shouted the suggestion "dildo factory."

The group, which comprised some of the best improvisers at the UCB Theatre at this time, did indeed set the show at a dildo factory, but none of the characters ever said the word "dildo," nor were any of the scenes about dildos. The reason I knew the show was taking place at a dildo factory was that they all would mime these horrendously long and elaborate dildos while they were having scenes about other things. They performed really impressive and precise object work while never mentioning the objects they were making.

Backline

There are two places for the backline: one, fittingly, is along the back. The other is along the sides, which keeps the back clear. Keeping everyone on the sides makes your set look more theatrical and professional, but, despite that, I like having people on the back. It's casual, friendly, and lets people get in the scene more quickly. It just seems friendly and more appropriate to the "jam" nature of improv.

Backline support should always start gingerly. Don't get in there until the principals (the people who started the scene) have made some decisions. Don't "fix" or steer from the back line; that's called being an "oppressive" back line, which is bad.

As the scene goes on, backline support is more allowed, and as a set goes on, backline support can start earlier and earlier in each scene.

Sweeps

Sweeps are great in how clear they are. There's no doubt a scene has ended when someone sweeps, but I find them odd and intrusive. They are also, along with tag-outs, one of the two frequently used improv conventions that non-improv audiences would never have seen before.

I prefer "soft edits." When a scene is done, a new person comes from the backline and begins another scene. You have to just be able to tell from context that this is a new scene rather than someone joining the previous one. It's usually not that hard to tell.

Walk-Ons

Walk-ons are friendly and supportive, like nice pats on the back. If you have an inkling, err on the side of doing them, as they usually don't hurt. If a team is playing too frantically, it helps to say "no tag-outs," but it's usually okay to let them still do walk-ons.

Tag-Outs

Tag-outs are expensive in that they destroy a whole scene for a joke, so be sparing. Don't do the first one too early in a scene, because there's no going back to a slower pace. If you're going to use one, the group should be ready to do a set of three, increasingly absurd. A tight, strong tag run can really make the room explode.

Tag-outs are best used right after someone has had a big reaction. You either tag out the other person and immediately try to provoke the same reaction, or you use tag-outs to segue to a new scene. If you're doing a montage or some form with a loose structure, and a scene is dying, you can do a tag-out to take a character to a new location and sort of start a new scene, without seeming like you're totally giving up on the previous one.

Sound Design

If there are two people doing a scene, but six people all piling on sound effects from the back, it's boring to watch. It probably means the backline is being oppressive and should back off, unless you're deliberately harassing the players on stage for fun, which I can't deny is a blast.

Extras

I've never been a fan of having actors flesh out a scene—say, if it's a party, and some people come from the backline to show there's other people at the party. To me it always feels like you're setting the expectation that they will be a big part of the scene. I think extras are generally distracting.

"We See"

Sometimes someone steps out and uses screenplay language to say something like, "We see this person is wearing an expensive watch." It's a dumb convention; don't ever do it, unless you're doing the movie form, which is what it was created for.

Swinging Doors

I haven't seen a non-ironic swinging door since 2002. Don't do them.

THE HAROLD

Openings

The opening destroys teams. It's about 10% of the Harold, but sucks up about 95% of a team's discussion of the Harold. You haven't been on a Harold team if you haven't spent hours and hours fretting over which opening to do and how to do it "right."

To avoid this destruction, a team should talk with their coach and be very specific about how they're going to do their opening. Set up a strict structure and follow it. Agree on the types of initiations you want to get out of it. Be narrow so you are on the same page. Usually with improv it helps to take a very "oh, I'll work with anything" kind of attitude, but not with Harold openings. Get specific.

Don't apologize to the audience for your opening being too weird. Just err on the side of keeping it short, and then very clearly use things from it. They'll accept it.

The simplest opening is a "monologue opening." You get a suggestion, and then three different members of the group tell a two-minute true story inspired by it. You pull scenes from the interesting parts of these stories. The monologue opening doesn't have enough group-work, however, to be a "real" opening. It's a training-wheels opening.

There are only three "real" openings: The Pattern Game, The Invocation, and a Sound and Movement. The Invocation is the easiest and was championed by Del. Sound and Movement doesn't give you any scene ideas but can be healing to a team that's having trouble getting along or having trouble committing, as I've said.

The Pattern Game is powerful, but it gets too absurd. Try to choose only the second-most absurd ideas you build. Say you have this little riff in a pattern game: "Cheese-stuffed pizza, cheese-stuffed kale, cheese-stuffed cheese!" Don't use "cheese-stuffed cheese"—it's one notch too silly. Good heavens, this paragraph is ridiculous.

Avoid rhyming and word play in pattern game—stuff like following up "Born free" with "Uh, porn free." You just broke the train of thought for a rhyme, and also, "porn free" isn't an idea: it only sounds like one.

First beats
Start with an idea, or at least start in the middle of something. Just starting a first beat with "Hey, how it's going?" is death to a Harold. It's okay in a scene that has no opening and where the discovery is a big part of the show, but in a Harold with an opening we want to hit the ground running with full initiations. They don't have to be funny, but it all works better if they are. It should be obvious how this initiation came from the opening.

Group games
These can be simple and fun. They don't need to be much more than a pattern. In the early days of the Harold, this was the spot for a short-form game, and it still works best if this scene feels like a break.

Because improvisers usually start with just two people in scenes, the biggest adjustment they need in order to do good group scenes is learning to do way less. You need 90% "yes" with 10% "and" to do a good group scene. Be ready to copy someone else's idea so there are not too many ideas in the scene.

The second group game should also take an idea from the opening, but it can also just speak to what feels like the dominant idea of the Harold. Look back and see if there's a common theme besides the suggestion, and use that to start your group game.

Second beats

These should not just continue the story. They should repeat and expand the weird philosophy from the first scenes.

A good strategy for second beats is to expand the world. If the second beat starts with a marathon runner insisting he be allowed to bring a chair with him, then we expand the world and cut to a meeting of an athletic commission trying to figure the best way to "test runners for chairs."

Third Beats

Don't plan your connections or force them. Ideally, they should surprise you. You just expand the world of your scenes, and the group will see a way to connect to the other scenes and characters. Make lots of choices as if you're starting a first scene, and you'll find a surprising way to connect to the other scenes.

Don't worry about theme and artsiness directly. Just try to be funny. The structure will take care of artistic depth. The structure forces you to revisit ideas and to connect them. You just try to steer the scenes towards funny ideas that don't break the reality.

THE MONOSCENE

The monoscene really works on non-improv audiences, because it does not contain any weird improv conventions like tag-outs or sweeps or openings. It feels like a play because it essentially is. If you're trying to win over a non-improv audience, try the monoscene!

There are two basic ways to do one:

1. Like a play, with one story that you keep fun via confessions and big endowments. If you're doing this, remember that whenever a character leaves the scene is the best time to endow them with a big gift. Right after Julia leaves, you say, "You know that Julia is getting really into karate?" Also remember to make big confessions when stuff is slowing down, especially ones that use loose ends. "I never told you this, but *I* was the one who bought the deer head."

2. Like a Harold, where you have three separate stories that we switch between until the end, when they all converge. This takes a bit more

discipline and needs to be agreed upon beforehand, but is pretty satisfying.

MONTAGE

Start slow, get faster. Hold off on the first tag-out for a few scenes.

It helps to make sure that the first three scenes are very different from each other.

Use different areas of your stage. That way when you return to a scene, you can indicate it clearly by going to that part of the stage.

After you're about two-thirds of the way through, you shouldn't really start any new scenes. Only re-use scenes and characters you've done already.

AN UNFAIR LIST OF PET PEEVES AND PERSONAL PREFERENCES

Emphasis on "unfair." This list is dumb.

PET PEEVES

No high-fiving.

Long-form improv has more unnecessary high-fiving than you'd ever imagine. Two characters agree to get ice cream and then high-five. They get each other's names wrong, then correct it, then high-five. It looks really weird, though I will admit no one seems to notice it. Except me. Even "bros" in improv high-five way more than regular bros. The only time a high-five is okay is when a character in improv just hit a home run.

No J names, especially "Janice"

This isn't a pet peeve as much as a phenomenon. The most common name given in improv is "Janice." By far. I'd say 50% of female characters in improv scenes are named Janice. And then the other J-names make up another 25% of characters. I guess J-names feel funny and interesting to people. "The Jenkins report" is another phenomenon, but I think people know about that one. "Janice" is everywhere but unnoticed. Disclaimer: I once belonged to a Harold team that used Janice so much we changed our name to Janice. No one liked it. The most common male name is "Gary."

Minimal pop culture references
Hearing the current movie du jour dropped into an improv scene starts to sound really clunky a few years into watching improv. I prefer made-up proper nouns. I still remember an improv scene some classmates of mine did about two people trying to guess the stars of the film "Two Jerks And A Stick," and an old UCB TourCo show where they talked about guys named Paul Boston and Ed Grapes.

"That's not what you said on your (dating website) profile."
Come on.

"That's the last time I get something from Craigslist."
You can do better.

No bowling alleys, no dentist appointments.
I could guess why (bowling means not looking at each other? Dentist requires someone to have their mouth full?) but for whatever reason, these scenes are often nightmares.

No board games
It's usually Monopoly or Battleship. That's weird, right? Monopoly I get, but who plays Battleship? Anyway, no one ever knows the rules and the scenes don't start for like five minutes. Weird exception: building houses of cards and Jenga both seem to work.

No pitch meetings/spitballing/ad guys
Right? "Guys, we need to come up with a new slogan for…"

Audiences giving as a suggestion whatever they see on stage, or a food
We have realized that 50% of all suggestions are foods, but another 40% are whatever the audience can see right in front of them. If half the guys are wearing plaid, they say "plaid." I've seen this multiple times, including last night. If someone has "Wildcats" on a shirt, they say "Wildcats." If more than two people have glasses, they say "glasses." It baffles me. You get one thing to do, audience, and you're already out of ideas? I guess this is also an argument against everyone wearing plaid and such, but still. The remaining 10% of suggestions are pop culture references.

PERSONAL PREFERENCES

Use names of friends from middle school
When you need a name, grab the actual first and last name of someone you knew in middle school. They're always specific and weird while still sounding true, because they are! Mark Chisholm. Chris Chamberlin. Paula Kubisek. Regina Glynn.

Everyone stand one half-step closer to each other
That makes it funnier. Another half-step is funnier still. For maximum funniness, use the Charlie Sanders "close eye" move, where you stand so your right eye is directly in front of the other person's left eye. It is intensely creepy and weirdly funny. It is not for strangers.

Specify a not-that-long-ago year
Explicitly set your scenes in a specific but non-notable year. "Hey, what do you want? It's 1997." This is like how *The Big Lebowski* came out in 1998 and made a big but largely unnecessary deal about being set in 1991. My favorite years for this are 1974, 1987, and 1995, for no reason at all.

Set your scenes in the third-most populated cities from any state
- Eugene, Oregon
- Rochester, New York
- Cincinnati, Ohio
- Tampa, Florida

Scenes where people are constantly preparing more and different foods in the kitchen while never addressing it or talking about it
I only saw this once, but I loved it.

Scenes where at least one person is holding their eyes 10% more open than normal.
Yep.

These words and terms, I love them: The commish. Dog war. Lock load and explode. Hewn. Brutal. Catbird seat. Not catbird seat, that's too much.
That's it.

FINAL
THOUGHTS

IS IMPROV A ROAD TO NOWHERE?

In September 2015 my friend Neil Casey got a job writing for *Saturday Night Live*. That's considered one of the plum jobs in all of comedy, and we were all excited for him.

Shortly after this, someone submitted a question to my improv blog titled: "*Is improv a road to nowhere?*"

The person was pointing out that Neil had done improv for years, yet it was probably a packet of written sketches that got him the *SNL* job, not a killer set in an improv show. If your goal is to write for a TV show or movie, he asked, then "*should one admit to themselves that as fun and enticing as improv is, if your ultimate goal is to achieve something like Neil, that improv should not be your main commitment?*"

It was a fair question. I had to admit that improv has seriously diminishing returns for stuff that translates into a paying job. At first it can definitely help you. It can connect you to a network of like-minded people and help you develop your voice and your confidence. But then, after some amount of time, you've met the people you're going to meet and your voice is as developed as it's going to be, so there's an argument to be made that you should get rid of all that time you're spending in rehearsal and write your own stuff.

I find that life isn't as clean as all that. You don't know which of your day's activities is going to flower forth into a huge part of your life later. When Neil started improv, he was a 20-year-old University of Delaware student commuting up to NYC to take classes with his friend Joe Wengert, and he loved it for its own sake. It clicked with him, and he followed the joy and love he felt for it. He met friends he liked and was happy spending his days doing it.

I highly doubt he was directly motivated by the idea of a possible writing job, except in an abstract "maybe someday" sense. He was thinking, "I hope I have fun in this 11 p.m. Owen Burke improv class show, in which I dress up like a superhero for an hour."

Doing those shows led him to being cast in other improv shows. He met friends and made sketch shows with them, as well as videos and character monologues and sometimes just silly running gags that existed only in conversations in the back room of McManus. Eventually, he taught classes and directed other people's sketch shows. Later he auditioned for roles on commercials and television shows.

Rarely would he be thinking, "I bet this will take me to *SNL*." Each of those steps was a joy unto itself. In a creative life, you don't always think, "What will this get me later?" You think, "What can I do *now* that is fun?" Yes and.

Improv doesn't try to lead you anywhere. It's just something that attracts certain kinds of people: comedy nerds who like performing, theater nerds who like comedy, and strange socially awkward list-makers with a good sense of the surreal.

One of the funniest things I have ever seen did not happen on a stage. In 2005 I went with a group of about 25 friends from the UCB Theatre to see a baseball game (the Mets hosting the Braves). Part way through the third inning, we noticed that our friend Rob Lathan was gone. "Did Rob leave?" we asked each other.

Then we spotted him all the way on the opposite side of the stadium. He was standing in an aisle of a completely empty section. A security guard walked up to him. We saw Rob show the guy his ticket. The guy pointed across the field at our section. Rob nodded and walked back into the stadium.

Then we saw him emerge into a different section, also very far away from his seat with us. Again, a security guard approached him. Again, Rob showed him his stub. Again, the guard pointed Rob toward his seat with us. Rob ducked into the stadium. We all started to giggle. *Rob is doing a thing.*

And for the next hour, we stopped watching the game and just watched Rob go to every single section in Shea Stadium, asking for directions to his seat. It kept getting funnier and funnier. We would roar with laughter each time he emerged in a new section.

Finally he came back to us. "Sorry," he said. "I got lost."

It was such an insane joke because he hadn't told anyone he was going to do it. What if none of us had noticed? In fact, how long had he been doing it before we noticed? Talk about a road to nowhere: that joke was done for 25 people who maybe wouldn't even see it.

About a year ago I was sitting in the Mustard Seed Cafe on Hillhurst Avenue in Los Angeles, reading a book. I heard someone say, "Can I get you anything?" and looked up to see a performer named Nate Lang, who I had performed with in New York City. I hadn't seen him in probably two years. He apparently had moved to LA (which I did not know), saw me in a diner, and walked in and pretended to be the waiter.

"Yeah, I'd like a cappuccino," I answered.

"Great. Be right back," Nate answered. And he walked out of the diner, crossed the street, and walked away. I haven't seen him since.

Isn't that a big reason why you do improv? To have people in your life that make you laugh and are weird in the way that you like?

The allure of success in entertainment is a tricky thing. Among the people who do improv are people who want to work in TV and movies. A small subset of those people make it. It's very easy to compare yourself against that track. Once you know someone who is successful on TV, it's natural to think, "Hey, why am I not on TV?"

I'm not opposed to career goals and success in the entertainment business.

It's good to have goals and to challenge yourself. It's good to make sure you're not stuck in a rut or avoiding something out of fear. Just as you want to make sure you're not avoiding acting choices out of fear in an improv scene, it's good to make sure you're not avoiding a creative challenge just because it takes you out of your comfort zone and asks you to devote time to submitting packets and trying to get auditions.

But commercial success is not the same as happiness. It's just what you're trying to do for a job.

Improv is something you do because you like it, not for what it gives you. I'm on an improv team with Katie Dippold, the screenwriter for *The Heat* and *Ghostbusters*, and I can assure you that she loves doing a good improv scene. It thrills her. She doesn't need it for her job, or for ideas, or for contacts. It's something that connects her to her true self.

One of my luckiest moments running classes for the UCB Theatre in New York happened in 2011 when Amy Poehler stopped by to take a look at our curricula.

Sitting in the UCB offices, I had a hunch that Amy still thought of herself as an improviser above other things. That she missed it and that she'd want a chance to be an improv teacher again. She's a famously good improv teacher.

I asked her if she would sub a class I was teaching because I was going out of town. I didn't really know her that well, but Amy is so friendly that after 10 seconds you feel like you know her and you find yourself comfortable asking things like that. She looked up and said, "Hmm. I really want to 'yes' you on that... so... well... yes!" That Saturday she taught my class, and 16 people got taught by one of the best comedians in the country. And yes, she was great.

She didn't do it to impress anyone or to further her career. She did it because she still thinks of herself as an improviser, and passing on the craft is something she believes in.

How do you measure how well you're doing in life? One time after a particularly bad improv set, I said to my friend Dyna Moe, "I don't know why I'm doing this. I'm bad at it! I'm wasting my time." She said to me, "Think of the other version of your life where you stayed working as a computer programmer. You'd still be in that cubicle, and you'd be wondering 'Could I have been a comedian? Could I have done it?' That person is so jealous of you, wishing that he could be where you are."

My friend reminded me of the strange creative life I've cobbled together. Jumping on a stage with genuinely talented people and fashioning a good show is an insanely thrilling trick that has not gotten old for me in 20 years.

Having friends in my life who fret about their creative projects, who love comedy and movies and theater, and who like making things is a hugely indulgent resource that I get to enjoy.

In the last month before writing this sentence, I put up a sketch show with two of my good friends, I directed and acted in a web series, I did a stand-up set, I recorded some episodes of a podcast, and I did several improv shows with people who are terrific on and off stage. I did this all in Los Angeles, which is a literal paradise of good weather. I've built a network of hilarious and fascinating friends. Some are famous; most are not. All of us have spent hours whooping and hollering in dance studios, trying to perfect a sound and movement, hoping it would get us out of our heads so we could make up a funny scene for an audience of 20 people.

There is a voice in my head that whispers, "This improv that makes you happy is a waste of your time." That voice is the enemy. Comparing yourself against the barometer of commercial success can be important to do as a motivator, but it isn't the only measure of success.

Road to nowhere! Good heavens. I mean, all roads lead nowhere. Try not to think about that. Spend your days in love with what you're doing as much as possible and thank the stars for your chances to do that. Be nice and honest and brave and hopeful and then let it go. The improv stages of Chicago and NYC and LA and elsewhere are filled with super talented people on roads to nowhere! I am one of those people!

If something is fun and enticing, you are victorious. You should keep doing that. If you're a zombie and going through the motions it's time to move on.

For me, I'm not in a cubicle giving my precious breath to a dumb company that I couldn't give a shit about, and so that's what I've got. It's a lot.

Improv is fun. Enjoy it. Something else I've now done: finished an improv book. Thank you for reading. See you around.

MORE ABOUT THE AUTHOR

I was born in 1970 in Dayton, Ohio, and then my family moved to Connecticut. A bunch of stuff happened, and then I took my first class at the Upright Citizens Brigade Theatre in New York City in 1999. I was a 29-year-old computer programmer who had never performed comedy.

As a kid I'd been funny, in an "honors student collecting old issues of *National Lampoon*" sort of way. My friends and I were into committed irony more than straight-up funniness, like playing handball but deciding you had to shout "Proust!" on every serve and refusing to come up with any explanation.

This didn't translate into professional aspirations of comedy. It almost seemed you'd have to be arrogant to assume you could do something like that. Without thinking about it too much, I assumed I'd slip into some kind of normal day job and make a family.

But that wasn't happening. The adult world was looking more and more stilted to me. New York City can be lonely. Everyone is busy with their agendas, and social circles are hard to penetrate. My co-workers were content to spend their days discussing sports scores and the tabloid story of the moment before rushing to their homes before eight.

And then I took that improv class.

It was partly the people that got me hooked. Unlike the people at my programming jobs, everyone there was interesting. There was a painter, a former *MAD Magazine* writer who had once interviewed the Clash, a production assistant from Troma Films, a few actors, and a cartoonist. There were two guys who'd gone to a Quaker high school and done a talk show for MTV as teenagers. One woman was a sex worker. Specifically, she was a "mistress" in a "dungeon," which was a sex club where she dressed up in garters and high heels and berated Wall Street investor types for money. She told us stories of her job very matter-of-factly.

Even the corporate people had a spark. There was a vice-president of an advertising company who was hilariously deadpan. In scenes, he always waited a second and a half before responding, which made everything he said deeply funny. He had impressively odd specifics like, "You make me feel like a hummingbird."

We stayed out until three in the morning after our first class. We got drunk and divulged personal stories about fist fights and losing our virginities. We discussed lots of movies and music. At one point the table sang along to A Tribe Called Quest's "Scenario," a song I had never heard.

This group asked very direct and personal questions. They were fun. They had a good sense of absurd declarations like, "There is no greater invention than sandwiches." One classmate was particular about making toasts. "To a new way of living," he would somberly say with each new round. Everyone was young or reckless enough to want to stay out too late.

Yes, the conversations often devolved into competitive games of one-upping the last ridiculous thing said, but the things said were specific, funny, and weird.

There were cool and interesting people in the world, and I now felt I was one of them.

But it was also the classes that got me hooked. Improv exercises felt like tests to see if I could shake off the dull world and connect with this new exciting one. I didn't think of scenes as funny—or not at first. I just tried to feel true or false. Performances were like referendums on how my personality was growing: if people laughed, then I was becoming the person I wanted to be.

Like all new improv students, I started hunting for good scene ideas everywhere. When an angry uncle described a politician as an "absolute top-drawer communist," instead of rolling my eyes, I tucked that phrase away. When I heard a shy receptionist at my work pipe up and seethe that she "hates parades," I took a moment to mentally record her sharp voice, her genuinely irritated expression.

I still do that. A few months ago a friend and I were texting, and he typed, "So what's the most physical pain you've felt in the last year?" Instead of wondering why he asked that, I just thought, "Hmm, that'd be a good thing to ask in a scene."

About a year into studying improv, I was visiting a friend who had a toddler. I tried reading a book to the toddler, and when he seemed bored I took it as a note. "I'm not being physically expressive," I thought, "just like my coach says." I then spent several minutes trying different silly voices and walks, trying to win over this three year old, all so I could potentially be funnier at my next improv show, which at that time would have been a class graduation show for about 10 people.

You start paying deeper attention to all of your own thoughts, looking for fun opinions you might drop into a scene. Do you prefer buttons or zippers, you ask yourself? Are door hinges essentially smug? You realize you actually have an answer to these ridiculous questions, and you hold onto them.

It wasn't just me. My whole little group got obsessed with improv. We'd practice outside of class once a week in my office. We saw shows at UCB two or three times a week. We went out drinking a lot and talked about improv and comedy and movies. Those of us with day jobs neglected them. Lots of couples got broken up as one half of them got too into improv.

And our improv, by the way, was bad.

But we kept going because the theater showed us improv that was cool and great. The founders of UCB—Matt Besser, Amy Poehler, Ian Roberts, and

Matt Walsh—were up-and-coming comedy stars with their own television show and small parts in movies. They did all the big comedy shows in New York. They were amazing enough that they drew swaths of amazing people from throughout the city to study with them.

Lots of the people I studied with in the early 2000s would go on to dominate American comedy for the next 15 years. But strangely, it felt like a long time before those of us on the lower rungs even thought about things like career success. Having brilliant comedians around just meant better teachers and coaches for our improv shows, and better people to impress in the audience. What I remember from the early 2000s are not scandalous exploits backstage, but struggling to do good things on stage, with a small room of amazing talent watching you and laughing when you got it right.

The quality of those shows at that time varied wildly, which was part of the fun. One instance of a weekly variety show called Bogus Sting featured legit great standup Todd Barry, then a dismal two-man improv team, then a guy declaring himself to be the mastermind behind the (then brand new) band The Strokes, who played a terrible version of their hit single on the piano but was overall kind of funny, then someone who said he had soccer great Pelé waiting in the green room to come talk to us, followed by a truly weird man who improvised a one-man dart game, which was somehow the funniest act of the night.

The theater moved from a 40-person space on the sixth floor of a warehouse (no elevator most of the time) to a 100-seat former strip club on a desolate side street (hard plastic molded seats, like an underfunded school) to a 220-seat playhouse right off Eighth Avenue (nice seats, but under a supermarket and with an enormous pillar smack dab in the middle of the front of the stage).

All the while, my friends and I made a name for ourselves in this society. We got made a house team, and some of us were hired as teachers. We aggressively befriended the incoming generations of students. We made a home for ourselves.

We got better.

ACKNOWLEDGMENTS

If I were to thank everyone who's helped me out during my time as an improviser, there would be hundreds of people to thank. I can't decide if it would be narcissistic to include them all or stingy to leave people out. Improv tells me to err on the side of saying yes, so here we go. Prepare for a steady pepping of silly proper nouns.

Editor: Malin von Euler-Hogan
Layout Designer: Nick Jaramillo
Cover Design: Maëlle Doliveux
Copy Editor: Alana Quirk
Author Photo: Jason Greene

People who read early drafts:
Elissa Bassist, Georgia Clark, Brigitte Dow, John Flynn, Brandon Gardner, Erin O'Brien, David Moldawer, Adam Pasulka, Shem Pennant, Tobias Sailer.

General advice and crucial encouragement on all things book-related: Jimmy Carrane, Jen Krueger, James Mulholland.

Lots of this book originally appeared as part of an improv blog I started in

2010 called "Improv Nonsense" (http://improvnonsense.tumblr.com). At one point, Tumblr listed it as a staff recommendation and I got 20,000 subscribers. Thank you to the many people who read the blog and who would contact me with thoughts and ideas about the posts.

Thanks to all my teachers and coaches: Sean Conroy, John Cameron Telfer, Rob McCaskill, Kevin Mullaney, Michael Delaney, Armando Diaz, Ali Farahnakian, Ian Roberts, Matt Walsh, Matt Besser, Amy Poehler, Seth Morris, Billy Merritt, Jackie Clarke, Anthony Atamanuik.

Thanks to Armando Diaz for putting me on my first house improv team. And then to the other Artistic Directors of the UCB Theatre in New York, each of whom cast me in shows and gave me advice and support: Kevin Mullaney, Owen Burke, Anthony King, Nate Dern, and Shannon O'Neill. Although they are all giants, I give special thanks to Anthony, who ran the place for seven years, turning a cool comedy clubhouse into a cool comedy metropolis, and being a good friend and improv nerd colleague throughout.

Thanks to Julie Brister for telling Kevin Mullaney I'd be a good teacher, and to Mullaney for listening to her. And then to Alex Sidtis, Susan Hale, and Joe Wengert for hiring me to run the New York school when Joe moved west in 2009. And to Johnny Meeks for letting me teach a lot at UCB-LA.

Thanks to John Frusciante for starting the UCB Comedy podcast, where he and I would talk to lots of great improvisers about improv theory. I stole lots of ideas from those interviews for this book. And thanks to podcast intern Cipha Sounds for being smart and funny, and for making us start the podcast a second time after we had let it retire.

Thanks to the Artistic Directors of UCB-LA for their support of many shows before and since I moved to Los Angeles: Neil Campbell, Alex Berg, and Mike Still.

To the many UCB old dogs for helping me out with so many shows in many ways: Alex Adan, Pat Baer, Shannon Coffey, Phil Del Costello, Chuck Dauble, Codi Fischer, Frank Garcia-Hejl, Rachael Mason, Achilles Stamatelaky.

I was lucky to come up at the UCB Theatre at a time when there was an explosion of talent. I got to play on teams with some of the best people you could imagine.

My first practice group, which never had a name but we informally called "Hit Show Club" since that was the name on the sign next to the office we'd sneak into in my office building (the roster changed a lot but the regulars were): Brian Berrebbi, Mike Bosniak, Pete Bosniak, Jake Fogelnest, Brett Gelman, John Gemberling, Rob Lathan, Mitch Magee, John Marshall, Josh Perilo, and Frankie Tartaglia.

Fire, Hot, Burn! My first UCB Theatre house improv team. When I got the news I had been added, I calmly walked out of my computer programming office and then ran up Ninth Avenue at top speed, unable to believe my luck. This team included Curtis Gwinn, Hilary Kimblin, Mike Bosniak, Josh Comers, Frank Shea, Hayden Ward, John O'Donnell.

Monkeydick: So sorry about the name. It was funny for a week and then we were together for four years. My practice group turned official house team. This team is where I was formed, and where I learned that the best way to be funny is to be yourself and be truthful at all costs. Brian Berrebbi, Neil Casey, Curtis Gwinn, Matt DeCoster, John Gemberling, Mitch Magee, Dyna Moe, Pete Bosniak, Rob Lathan, Andy Rocco. And Jane Borden, Ed Herro, and Sara Jacobs too! And Billy Merritt for coaching us a million times.

Thanks to sketch geniuses Joe Wengert and Neil Casey for asking me to direct their first sketch shows at the theatre, which let me be part of their inspiring, surreal mindset, and allowed us all to become Actual Friends. In addition, thanks to Game Face, the sketch group formed by Joe, Neil, and I with Rob Lathan and Mitch Magee. The six or seven sketch shows (!) we made in 2003 and 2004 were an insane joy.

Primal Bias: My brother's indie team (meaning we were not affiliated with any theater), which was my first team of all friends, which made all of our shows a joy to do. Kevin Cragg, Kevin Hines, Dave Lombard, Porter Mason, Gavin Speiller, Erik Tanouye, Silvija Ozols, and sometimes we'd trick Ashley Ward into joining, too.

Thanks to Terry Jinn for The Project, an improv show that asked people to create so many fun and happy improv teams, including Primal Bias.

Team Brooklyn: When the UCB tried to colonize hipster Williamsburg they sent us, the house team players who lived there. An insanely fun group that performed all shows at top volume, top speed, and great fun. Will Becton,

Jeff Campbell, Brian Finkelstein, Mark Sam Rosenthal, Charlie Sanders, and, even, for one quick show (the day before he got *The Daily Show*) Ed Helms.

The Brothers Hines: I feel I could write a second book on how lucky I am that my brother Kevin also fell in love with improv at the same theatre, and that we got to do so many shows as a duo. Improv gives you a special kind of intimacy and trust with your teammates, and to get that with my own brother is one of the things I'm most grateful for. Hey, and we were funny, too! Also thanks to brother Brian, who we convinced to do shows with us a few times, too, and who's been a supportive friend during all of this silly improv endeavor.

Arsenal: From the ashes of Monkeydick, I got moved to a great team of great people that we all soon destroyed. Rob Webber, Flynn Barrison, Nate Shelkey, Maggie Kemper, Rebekka Johnson, David Martin, and Porter Mason.

Strongers: A mastermind scheme of Terry Jinn and Ptolemy Slocum that let me do shows with an amazing group. Elna Baker, Terry Jinn, Ellie Kemper, Andrew Secunda, Ptolemy Slocum, Shelly Slocum, and Kevin Townley.

1985: The most fun I've ever had on an improv team. We'd all been around the block and learned to have fun at all costs. Flynn Barrison, Sue Galloway, Birch Harms, Adam Pally, Porter Mason, Ben Rodgers, Charlie Sanders, Risa Sang-urai, Gavin Speiller, Erik Tanouye, and Jim Santangeli.

The Stepfathers: The best improv team I'll ever be on, performing for the best audience, the Friday night crowd at UCB New York. Michael Delaney, Alexandra Dickson, Don Fanelli, Chris Gethard, Jordan Klepper, Bobby Moynihan, Shannon O'Neill, Silvija Ozols, Connor Ratliff, Andrew Secunda, and Zach Woods. Not to mention the comedy giants who left the team before I got there: Billy Merritt, Christina Gausas, Brian Huskey, and Peter Gwinn.

Thanks to Neil Casey for not only being on a bunch of the teams listed here but also for working with me to co-write and co-star in our sketch show, Small Men. From Neil and director Michael Delaney, I learned how to write sketch all over again with this show, and it's my proudest comedy achievement.

Your Fucked Up Family: The Los Angeles descendants of Death by Roo Roo. Fast, smart, funny, and fearless. These guys added me to the roster a month

BEFORE I moved, which made the terrifying life change of switching coasts so much easier. Dan Black, Neil Casey, Jon Gabrus, John Gemberling, Jeff Hiller, Dan Klein, Pam Murphy, Gil Ozeri, Adam Pally, and Mike Still.

The Smokes: My permanent improv home in LA, filled with friends from the old days of UCB. Getting added to this team is one of the luckiest and happiest improv things to have happened to me. Susannah Becket, Neil Casey, Eugene Cordero, Katie Dippold, Brian Gallivan, Chris Kula, Billy Merritt, Tricia McAlpin, Joe Wengert, and Jim Woods.

Along the way I've been on so many indie improv groups I literally cannot remember them all. Some that stand out: TJ Monkeys (Yes, I was on the team—with Porter Mason and Flynn Barrison), Distant Cousins (with Phil Jackson), Fuckable (with Mel Cowan and Jonny Svarzbein), Matador (with Mel Cowan, Holly Laurent, and Jet Eveleth), Bad at Parties (with Jen Krueger), Byer and Hines (with Nicole Byer), and a bunch of others.

Some of the great improv and sketch teams I got to coach: Police Chief Rumble, Twelve Thousand Dollars, Whorenado, iBadger, Mixtape '98, Bastian, Neighbor Boy, Never Never, Cardinal Redbird, Oh, Brother! and Nephew.

Thanks to Todd Bieber for teaching me how to make comedy videos. Thanks to Sean Clements for writing amazing scripts and then letting Todd and me bring them to life.

Thanks to Sam Reich and everyone at the website CollegeHumor for hiring me to act in and direct their videos, and for proving to the New York comedy scene that people can be talented, professional, and genuinely nice. Special thanks to Elaine Carroll for casting me as "Fat Professor" in her hilarious Very Mary-Kate videos.

And a final, special thanks to all the teachers I got to hire at UCB-NY, because it meant I got to watch them teach and steal their ideas.

Thanks to everyone who let me quote their scenes as examples:
Mano Agapian, Stephanie Allyne, Frank Banz, Stephan Bekiranov, Alex Berg, Brock Bivens, Lilan Bowden, Somner Branham, Heather Campbell, Neil Campbell, Brad Cameron, Jimmy Carrane, Toni Charline, Rhona Cleary, Christopher Corbin, Dennis Curlett, Danny Cymbal, Jon Daly, Michael Delaney, Todd Fasen, Casey Feigh, Cissy Fenwick, Alex Fernie,

Michael Gardner, Brett Gelman, John Gemberling, Seth Gilbert, Rene Gube, Curtis Gwinn, Michael Hanggi, David Harris, Mary Holland, Cory Jacob, Cody Kopp, Chris Kula, Lauren Lapkus, Raymond Lew, Dan Lippert, Jon Mackey, James Mannion, Hillary Matthews, Adam McCabe, Ryan Meharry, Billy Merritt, Colin McGurk, Gwen Mesco, Kristina Nikolic, Rose O'Shea, Jake Pinton, Zach Pyke, Jacob Reed, Andy Rocco, Mary Sasson, Betsy Sodaro, Max Sosna-Spear, Ryan Stanger, Drew Tarver, Ruha Taslimi, Michelle Thompson, Lisa Timmons, Paul Welsh, Robert Woo, Zach Woods, Heather Woodward.

Thanks to the people who've hired me to come to their towns and teach: Shem Pennant and Carleen Macdermid of C3? (See Three Something) in London, Garrett Palm with Curious Comedy Theater in Portland, Tobias Sailer of AMS! Improv in Bremen, Han Tang and Duo with Mah Wah Theatre in Beijing, Jakob Grotewohl and Noah Telson of Comedy Café in Berlin, James Clark with Governor Jack in Denver.

And a final, special thanks to Michael Delaney. Delaney is the best improviser I have ever seen, was my teacher, and later was my teammate on the Stepfathers. When I ran the school, Delaney was the one who was most likely to call me and insist that things could be taught better. Those conversations were so helpful and illuminating, and are directly or indirectly the source of every good idea in this book. The UCB Theatre would not have been as good without him, and I feel lucky to have gotten to work with him for so long.

And thanks, of course, to you and everyone who reads this book.

CPSIA information can be obtained
at www.ICGtesting.com
Printed in the USA
LVOW04s0209120916

504207LV00009B/180/P

9 780982 625729